NO NUMBERED RUNWAYS

Jack Schofield

NO
NUMBERED
RUNWAYS

*Floatplane Pioneers
of the West Coast*

SONO NIS PRESS
Winlaw, British Columbia

Copyright © 2004 by Jack Schofield

**National Library of Canada Cataloguing in
Publication Data**

Schofield, Jack, 1927-
    No numbered runways : floatplane pioneers of
the West
Coast / Jack Schofield.

ISBN 1-55039-146-1

    1. Floatplanes—Pacific Coast (British
Columbia)—History.
2. Air pilots—Pacific Coast (British Columbia)—
History. I. Title.

TL539.S36 2004   387.7'3347'09227111
    C2004-902189-3

Sono Nis Press most gratefully acknowledges the
support for our publishing program provided by the
Government of Canada through the Book Publishing
Industry Development Program (BPIDP), The
Canada Council for the Arts, and the British
Columbia Arts Council.

Editing by John Eerkes-Medrano
Cover photo by Rich Hulina © 2003

Published by
SONO NIS PRESS
Box 160
Winlaw, BC V0G 2J0

1-800-370-5228

books@sononis.com
www.sononis.com

Printed and bound in Canada by Friesens Printing.

CONTENTS

Preface   6

Introduction: Something About Floatplanes   7

1   We Remember Ginger   11

2   The Short, Furious History of Pioneer Airways   27

     Hangar Flying: Journey Log—June 15, 1939   37

3   The Press and Paddy Burke   41

4   The Great Mush   55

5   The Whistling What?   61

     Hangar Flying: Flights of Fashion   69

6   This Sylvester Was No Pussycat   75

7   No Tie No Fly   87

8   The Chicken Hawk Airline   97

     Hangar Flying: Sex and the Single Engine   109

9   Paper Bag Pilot   119

10   Keeping the Old Crate New   131

"There I was, upside down, with nothing on the clock but the maker's name."

This is a traditional opener for pilots recounting their aerial adventures. They call it "Hangar Flying," and the term has persisted since the earliest days of aviation. Every pilot is guilty of telling tall tales and true; some of those tales are included here to provide the reader with an insider's feel for this adventurous industry.

PREFACE

They flew their aircraft low during good-weather days, committing the uncharted shoreline to memory—a memory that would guide them, during winter's low visibility, from the fog and drizzle of the rain forest. They stayed alive by learning quickly: reading the water beneath them for wind direction and strength, staying clear of the turbulent lee side of mountain peaks, landing into black gusts they called "cat's paws" when the winds seemed to gust from all directions.

These coastal navigators did not speak of bearings to or magnetic headings from, as is the tradition of mariners. Instead, seaplane pilots referenced homely checkpoints such as "that big white rock on the beach" or a significant cedar snag that pointed out their path. They did all this from a not-uncommon altitude of 50 feet between their aircraft's pontoons and the raging coastal waters. These were the pioneer aviators of Canada's west coast, whose flying skills and local knowledge of the coast's myriad inlets and waterways brought the miners, loggers, fishermen, prospectors, preachers, prostitutes, misfits and visionaries to the hinterland.

They started flying into the bush in the late 1920s, and continue to do so today. These pilots are fired with the adventure of their pursuit and an inexplicable love of flight. Their communality crosses generations and is particularly evident among aviators who combine their passion with their entrepreneurial skills to create the airline businesses that serve this unique wilderness market. Although many survived the hazards of flying, proficiency in the cockpit did not guarantee business success—the aircraft of one venture was often later seen repainted in the colour of another man's dream.

In these pages you will find the exciting stories of some early and latter-day entrepreneur-aviators whose floatplanes tracked the coastal wilderness. Their exploits—some amazing, some hilarious and others tragic—shaped the aviation history of Canada's west coast.

SOMETHING ABOUT FLOATPLANES

Almost all of the flying history of Canada's west coast took place "on floats." Readers unfamiliar with the operational characteristics of float-planes versus their wheel-equipped cousins may find the following information helpful.

When taxiing on the water, airplanes mounted on pontoons or floats are manoeuvred in a manner best compared to a ship under sail. An aircraft's vertical stabilizer provides directional stability when flying, acts as a sail during water handling, and awakens the aircraft's innate desire to "weather-cock" into wind. Drawing only a foot or so of water, a seaplane is at the will of the wind, and the stronger the wind the greater the plane's desire to swap ends. Using power during water handling is counterproductive, and it is usually restricted to the actual takeoff or to what is known as "step-taxiing." The "step" on an aircraft's float is a unique design feature that allows an aircraft to make the change from displacing water to planing on the surface. Taxiing "on the step" is the use of near-takeoff power in order to "motorboat" at high speed across open water. When docking the aircraft, the pilot throttles back to idle and steers with the craft's retractable water-rudders, which are mounted on the stern of the floats. These rudders are integrated with the linkage to the air rudder, and the pilot's feet perform the steering action.

Very strong winds sometimes require the pilot to sail the plane backwards. In such circumstances he can control the backward speed only by bursts of power to slow down the rearward drift. Sometimes he will open and close doors on either side of the aircraft—an interesting way to steer the tail around. Backing onto a dock will often accelerate the pilot's aging process and is not a normal procedure.

Taxiing crosswind over swells also adds a new dimension to floatplane handling. The rocking action imposed on the aircraft by those wind-driven swells causes the wings to present themselves, alternately, at a higher angle of attack to the fast-moving air. This can lead the upgoing wing to get the idea it should be flying, while the downgoing wing, denied that flying urge, goes for a swim. Under such circumstances the pilot gets to inspect the bottom of his floats, often for the first time, while seated on the spreader bars between them, waving for help.

Topographical features of the surrounding land mass of a bay, cove, river or inlet create wind and water conditions unique to that specific area. Pilots with local knowledge learn to anticipate these and actually use the local phenomenon to their advantage when landing and taking-off. As the title of this book suggests, there is no ground support for seaplanes that fly the coast—no navigational aids, no one looking out for you—*no numbered runways*—it is all pilot decision-making when flying on floats. The insurance companies know this and get very skittish about insuring pilots who have few flying hours off the water. Strangely, this is not the position of the licensing authorities, who will endorse a pilot for operating on floats with proof of a mere five hours of instruction. But this pilot will never get a job until he logs at least a thousand hours. This results in a Catch-22: how does he log a thousand hours without getting a job?

Although seaplane pilots today are faced with the same operating parameters as their counterparts had in 1920, there are some notable differences. The early pilots didn't have any maps of what was mostly an uncharted area, and being few in number they needed to be familiar with much more territory than do today's "coast dogs." Those real bush pilot pioneers didn't have aircraft designed specially for the job, such as today's Short Take-off and Landing (STOL) de Havilland Beavers and Otters. Nor did they have radio communication systems or en route fuelling facilities.

One thing that remains a common need of seaplane pilots across the years is dry floats. Water continues to weigh ten pounds per gallon, and leaky floats can seriously alter the weight and balance of an aircraft, even sink it if those so-called watertight compartments are compromised. Like the *Titanic*, pontoons are compartmentalized for safety's sake—as many as eight compartments per pontoon. But, unlike the case with the *Titanic*, the bulkheads go all the way up to the deck. Continual punishment from takeoffs and landings on rough water takes its toll on the sheet metal seams of the best pontoons, and leakage will occur. Pilots become adept at pumping out the float bilge, particularly at the "step" compartment, where the sheet metal work becomes intricate. Small bilgeing ports are located atop the float deck for each of these compartments. To keep water from slopping into these compartments, the bilgeing holes are plugged with those red, white and blue rubber balls used in the child's game of Jacks—they are a perfect fit. Crows are attracted by the balls' bright colours and sometimes peck these stoppers out and carry them away. If the crows don't succeed in stealing the balls, very hot weather expands the float compartment and the plugs pop out while the plane sits in the sun at the dock. In either case, it is accepted in the industry that you can tell a seasoned floatplane pilot from the fact that he often complains of having more than once lost his balls.

9

1

WE REMEMBER GINGER

Fighting in the trenches of the Great War at a mere 15 years of age, this regimental mascot turned sniper was a deadly shot with a Ross rifle. Awarded his commission at age 17 and twice wounded in the trenches before remustering into the Royal Flying Corps, Russell Leslie "Ginger" Coote was considered a "natural" pilot—a reputation that endured for 40 years, as he laid the foundation of aviation history on British Columbia's coast.

Grinning down from the open cockpit of the little biplane, Ginger Coote felt a familiar rush of exhilaration. He fired the throttle to the gate and pulled the plane's nose up until the lower wing tip stood at right angles to the horizon. As the craft hung for a moment on its propeller, Ginger stabbed on full right rudder and thrilled himself and his father, watching from below, as the plane's nose traded blue sky for a view of trees rushing up at incredible speed. Crossing the horizon again, he powered off and eased out of what he called a hammerhead stall. Now, speeding across the rooftop of his house, waggling his wings in response

to the frantic waves from family on the ground, he dove the Eaglerock biplane between the trees, levelling out mere inches from the gravel road. Sighting through the cross of flying wires in front of him, Ginger chased through the dustball made by a Ford Model T on the road ahead.

The thrill he felt as he zoomed over the car and its startled driver was mixed with memories of his recent days in the Royal Flying Corps. He had flown an SE5 fighter back then and would have been going quite a bit faster and making a lot more noise than he did today in the Eaglerock. The SE5 also had a Vickers machine gun

12

mounted topside on the upper wing.
Crack shot that he was, Ginger could
have reduced Curly Evans's Model T
Ford to scrap iron, but the young pilot's
thoughts were far from warlike as he
creamed past his startled but now
grinning and waving neighbour and
flung his exciting new airplane into the
summer sky of 1930.

In the trenches of France at the
tender age of 15, Russell Leslie "Ginger" Coote had been advanced from a
bugle boy to a sniper with the Canadian Expeditionary Force's 47th
Battalion. His outstanding marksman-
ship placed him in the thick of the
action for the next three years. Ginger's

expertise with the special telescopic
sight-mounted Ross rifle brought him
to the attention of his commanders and
resulted in his being commissioned as a
sub-lieutenant at age 17. Sub-lieuten-
ants didn't last long in the First World
War, as they were the first over the
top, armed only with a pistol, leading
their troops to inevitable slaughter.
Ginger was lucky. Twice wounded
during his three years in the trenches,
he survived injuries at Vimy Ridge and
again at Lens, in 1917. In the wound-
ing at Lens, he was left for dead in a
shell hole in no man's land. A close
friend, Benny Benfield, undertook a
dramatic rescue: Benfield had marched
two German prisoners at gunpoint out
to the shell hole where Ginger was
lying. The enemy held their fire, afraid
of killing their own people, and Ginger
was dragged to safety.

The young officer was shipped off
to Britain to recuperate. While hospi-
talized in England, he swore never to
return to that hellish life in the
trenches. The sound of aircraft at a
nearby airport gave him the idea to
remuster into the Royal Flying Corps
(RFC)—a decision that would influ-
ence his life forever and have a lasting
effect on the history of aviation in
British Columbia. The 18-year-old
proved to be a natural pilot and was
soon awarded his RFC wings. Follow-

Ginger, pictured here in the rear cockpit of his Eaglerock biplane, started what survives to this day as the Chilliwack Flying Club. When he became busy with his airline, Bridge River & Cariboo Air Services, he gave this airplane to the club. It ended up in the trees near Yale, B.C. GINGER COOTE SCRAPBOOK, COURTESY MOLLY COOTE

ing his flight training, he was transferred to a coastal reconnaissance squadron, where he flew the first-line fighter of 1918—the SE5.

With the war winding down and finally coming to an end on November 11, 1918, Ginger signed on for an extra two years' service in the newly created Royal Air Force (RAF). His military experiences undoubtedly shaped his future, honing the flying skills that would soon be his fortune. Early in 1920, he quit the RAF and returned to his family home in Chilliwack.

This 21-year-old war veteran made a valiant attempt to settle down in what was considered a respectable occupation—tilling the soil in B.C.'s lush Fraser Valley. He married Helen Chadsey, a former schoolmate from Chilliwack, and threw himself into this earthbound occupation, discovering very quickly that he was not cut out for

the farmer's life. He sold the farm and took a short-lived sales position with the Imperial Oil Co.

Flying airplanes was proving to be a hard act to follow, and Ginger's attempt at being employed in a "normal" job was very short-lived. He scraped his money together and bought a pretty little Alexander Eaglerock biplane, flying it into the Chadsey family pastures, where he started what survives to this day as the Chilliwack Flying Club.

The young pilot was now back in his element—doing snap rolls and stall turns just like in the old days. He was also teaching his friends and neighbours how to fly and, on the side, chartering his flying services to miners and hunters and sightseers who were looking for a quick way through the mountains into the Cariboo country.

While Ginger was having fun,

The Ryan Brougham CF-ATA was a design spinoff from the *Spirit of St. Louis*, the aircraft flown solo by Charles Lindbergh across the Atlantic Ocean just three years before this photo was taken. Ginger's first commercial airplane burned to the ground at Quesnel five months after the formation of his Bridge River & Cariboo Air Services.

GINGER COOTE SCRAPBOOK, COURTESY MOLLY COOTE

making a modest living from training students and performing charter flights, his long-time friend, Neal "Curly" Evans, saw a bigger future for Ginger and his airplane. Curly had a little trucking business hauling freight and workers from Vancouver into the Bridge River country. Mining was a boom industry in Bridge River, with Bralorne and Pioneer Gold Mines and the sluicing operation at Minto becoming big customers of Curly's company, Neal Evans Transportation Co. Operating trucks out of Shalalth and over Mission Mountain into these mine sites was a hazardous business; the road was not much more than a pack trail in those days. The steep grade and the near-vertical cliffs on each side of the mountain road were a challenge to both truck and driver at any time of year, but with the winter snows they were a frightening undertaking. Curly, ever the businessman—at least, com-

pared with Ginger—saw airplanes as the answer for passenger service and for carrying some of the freight his company was hauling. After looking at Ginger's Eaglerock biplane, Curly realized it would take a more substantial plane to do the job.

Curly Evans didn't have much trouble convincing Ginger that they should form an airline. The two men located a U.S.-registered Ryan Brougham aircraft in Bellingham, Washington, and purchased it in June 1932. Registered in Canada as CF-ATA, the Ryan was the commercial version of the *Spirit of St. Louis*, the aircraft that Charles Lindbergh had just flown across the Atlantic Ocean. Although it was a good plane for charter work, embodying all the available technology of 1932, it was not designed to be mounted on floats. The two men planned to operate on wheels in the summer and on skis in the winter into the Cariboo area, where there were now a few designated airports and many open fields suitable for landing. They formed their company under the name of Bridge River and Cariboo Air Services, the company registration indicating that Ginger's prestigious father, Lieutenant-Colonel A. Leslie Coote, was a director. Presumably, Dad kicked in some of the money for the purchase of the Ryan aircraft. Considering that 16 months would pass before Ginger and Curly obtained their operating certificate for the airline, it can be guessed that they performed what the industry now calls "chisel charters" for that period. Private aircraft are not allowed to fly for hire, so it is likely that the Ryan's services were billed out as freight hauling by Neal Evans Transportation during this waiting period.

Obtaining a charter and scheduled airline licence was no small feat. There were many hoops to jump through, as the government of Canada was itself in some confusion as to how to handle civil aviation. In the past, Ottawa had been more involved with trains than planes and had allowed the military to look after aviation licensing and regulations. Now, with the appointment of 18 aviation inspectors who were sent out to all of Canada's provinces and territories, the newly formed

Civil Aviation Division of the Department of Transport was planning to place more control on private and commercial aircraft operators. New regulations were being drafted to control this fast-growing industry, and Ginger, along with others in the business, would be confronted by the recently appointed B.C. inspector, R. Carter Guest. Arriving on the scene in 1930, Guest would demand aviators' compliance with those few regulations already in place and impose a new consideration of safety on the flying business—the days of barrel rolls down Main Street were officially over.

Bridge River and Cariboo Air Services came into existence October 3, 1933. The airline was not the first commercial air service in B.C., but it

15

The famous Fairchild, CF-AUX, which figured in many of Ginger's rescues. The rag-and-tube aircraft is pictured here at Gunn Lake on the occasion of a family picnic. AUX came to a sticky end in the trees at Franklin River, in Alberni Inlet, in June 1938.

16

would become a principal player in the exciting future of this industry. At the outset, the company was fraught with "typical" airline problems. The Ryan aircraft burned to the ground at Quesnel during an engine preheating, only five months after the company's inauguration. A Gypsy Moth DH60M biplane on floats was acquired to bridge the gap and held the airline together until a more suitable aircraft could be found. Ginger soon located what was to be the most famous of his airplanes—famous because both he and that aircraft soon appeared repeatedly on the front pages of the three Vancouver newspapers. His local fame resulted from the performance of feats of mercy, police support and explora-

tion that made him the darling of the press for many years.

Mounted on floats, the new aircraft was a high-wing monoplane built by Fairchild Aircraft in Longueuil, Quebec. Designated as a model 51A and referred to as rag-and-tube design, the fabric-covered, steel-tube-constructed Fairchild bore the 30-inch letters CF-AUX on its dark-blue, slab-sided fuselage. The demand for this floatplane for charters into the lakes and inlets of the coastal area far outstripped the earlier work performed by the wheel-equipped Ryan, and Ginger's airline was now truly launched.

Ginger Coote became the only bush pilot in the sky, according to kids

These pilots spent weeks searching for AUX but had to give up without locating the missing aircraft with its pilot and three passengers. Ginger was particularly devastated that his good friend, Mrs. G. Nicholson, the Zeballos health nurse, was aboard. ELWOOD WHITE PHOTO

growing up in British Columbia during the early 1930s. Knuckling down to a hot game of marbles on the grounds of Vancouver schoolyards, more than one young plane buff would pause to follow the descent of the Fairchild or, later, Ginger Coote Airlines' Fox Moth, as it let down to join the circuit for the river at Sea Island airport. It was a rare sight in those days to see more than one plane in the sky at the same time, so the kids figured it was always Ginger Coote at the controls. In the classroom, when they heard the passing drone of a plane, a knowing look would be exchanged between these would-be aces: "There goes old Ginger again."

These air-minded youngsters had never seen "old Ginger," but they were certain he would be decked out in bulky flying togs with helmet and goggles and, of course, he would wear a smear of castor oil across his handsome brow. They imagined him in the air from dawn 'til dark, arrowing through the coastal rain storms, beating his way up the shoreline in near-zero visibility—rushing that lifesaving serum to some remote coastal community. In their young minds, Ginger Coote was the ultimate hero. They came by their hero-worship honestly; the press had, by this time, dubbed him the "Mercy Pilot" because of the many people he had rescued

from the bush. Ginger's job of flying floatplanes was, to these youngsters, the greatest act of heroism. More than being a fireman or policeman, many a boy in those days wanted to be just like Ginger Coote—a famous bush pilot.

The kids were wrong about the flying togs and the castor oil; Ginger was well known for flying in street clothes, wearing his trademark fedora hat. As for the castor oil, that was something from the past used in the Rhone rotary engines that powered the aircraft Ginger might have flown in the recent war. But those kids were right about one thing—Ginger was famous. Hardly a day went by without some mention of this popular folk hero in Vancouver's *Daily Province* or *Sun* newspapers or the *News Herald*. The press of the day were fascinated with what they termed "mercy flights," and Ginger performed a lot of them: it was

17

Left: The U.S. Coast Guard sent an aircraft to assist in the search for Ginger's missing Fairchild. This was not an uncommon gesture. GINGER COOTE SCRAPBOOK, COURTESY MOLLY COOTE

Right: AUX was found by a survey team one year after it went missing. The bodies and wreckage were removed by Ginger and a rescue team. R. CARTER GUEST COLLECTION

calculated by one of the newspaper pundits that Ginger had saved more lives than had been lost in all B.C. aviation accidents up to that date.

On October 27, 1938, a British newspaper, the *Birmingham Daily Mail* praised Ginger in an article that attested to the B.C. aviator's growing worldwide fame: "R.L. Coote, better known as 'Ginger,' is British Columbia's 'Mercy Flyer' and possibly might even be reckoned as No. 1 Mercy Flyer of all Canada." The article went on at length to describe the flying career of this RFC-trained pilot and his near-single-handed role in the early development of commercial aviation in British Columbia and the Yukon.

In local newspapers, the appearance of the name "Ginger" was all it took—British Columbians were on a first-name basis with their favourite

pilot. *Daring Rescue by Ginger Saves Trappers—Coote Finds Missing Man—Tragedy Told by Ginger of Trappers Dead in Cabin—Ginger's Moth Back in Service—Ginger Installs Radios in Planes*—whatever happened to Ginger Coote was grist for the newspaper's mill. The most famous of all Ginger's exploits was his aerial search for two desperadoes who robbed the Hudson's Bay Co. post at Fort Nelson and made off down the Liard River in canoes with $30,000 worth of furs. The police engaged Ginger, and soon the peripatetic CF-AUX was in hot pursuit, with the press reporting the chase in serialized form. Needless to say, the airborne "white hats" won the day and the desperadoes were clapped in irons. And guess whose handsome, grinning face appeared on the front page of every newspaper?

Ginger Coote Airways' new Norseman, AZE, had an engine failure near Gower Point, at the mouth of Howe Sound. Ginger paddled it to False Creek, arriving in the dead of night. Anxious staff were relieved when his only passenger showed up at 2 A.M. carrying the aircraft's mailbag. PETER CORLEY-SMITH COLLECTION

It could be said that Ginger never attended a temperance meeting, and there is evidence that he was never far away from a 40-pounder of his favourite Monogram Rye—a habit he learned in France to maintain his sanity in the hell of the trenches. Cecil Pickell, an air engineer who flew with Ginger on several occasions, recalled: "We were heavily loaded, attempting a takeoff, when Ginger had to abort the attempt. While taxiing back for another try, he turned to me and said that he knew what the problem was— we were just too heavy. With that, he reached under his seat, pulled out a bottle of whisky and took a swig out of it. 'That'll lighten the load,' he said, and sure enough we got off that time."

The memories of friends and relatives are that whenever Ginger was present, a good time was had by all.

Margaret Rutledge (Fane), who worked for Ginger during the Zeballos gold rush, tells of the day he landed the Norseman CF-AZE at Gun Lake, where he had built a little cabin for weekend fishing trips and family outings. Approaching the seaplane dock a little too fast, Ginger had jumped down onto the pontoon and called out to his wife, who was standing on the dock. "Throw me that rope," he yelled, gesturing to a rope coiled on the dock's tie-up cleat. Ginger's wife scooped up the rope as requested and threw it to him as he came drifting alongside the dock. To everyone's amazement, the rope was not attached to the dock and the plane just sailed on by, making for the beach, with Ginger holding the loose end and grinning from ear to ear.

"Ginger laughed so hard, he lost his footing and fell into the water." Margaret smiled as she recounted the story. "He continued to laugh as he bobbed around in the lake." Ginger couldn't swim, and Margaret became concerned that he was shipping a lot of water because his mouth was open from all that laughing, and his boots were filling with water and weighing him down alarmingly. "He was going down for the third time when I just dove in off the plane and grabbed him and dragged him with me to the beach,"

"Did you build that yourself?" might well be the question, but the ugly Fleet Freighter was very innovative despite its ungainly appearance. The short-lived aircraft was flown by Ginger, Sheldon Luck and Grant McConachie on the famous Kamloops inaugural mail run—a joint venture with United Air Transport that heralded the beginning of Yukon Southern Air Transport. PETER CORLEY-SMITH COLLECTION, B.C. PROVINCIAL ARCHIVES

she said. "Ginger couldn't stop laughing as he choked and sputtered while watching helplessly from the beach as the Norseman drifted down the lake into the overhanging trees. He was a great guy."

The "great guy" had some adventures that were not for public consumption. As one wag put it, "Ginger flew out to a lot of traplines—one of them was his own." The details of his three marriages—both the consummation and the dissolution—made the papers, but only one other of Ginger's romances found its way into the public realm. The press had a field day with what it labelled "The Bleeding Heart Case," in which one Marie-Antoinette Nolan sued Ginger for $20,000, claiming breach of promise. It seems that Ginger, in the heat of the moment, had convinced Marie-Antoinette that he was single and that

he would happily change that status in consideration of her performing a more immediate need. Like her namesake, this Marie-Antoinette seemingly lost her head, and she presented the court with her four-year-old child as proof of the dalliance with Ginger. Despite the absence of DNA testing in that day, the lady did not fail to convince the court that there was some substance to her claim. Marie-Antoinette was awarded damages, but not to the extent of the suit. The sum of $3,380 was levied against the province's aerial folk hero, but no explanation was given of how that odd amount was determined. It was thought that the presiding judge was a fan of the flying folk hero and had softened the blow.

As the airline expanded into new areas, it became obvious that the Bridge River and Cariboo name was becoming inappropriate. What better name to bestow on the company than that of Ginger himself, who was now famous? Ginger Coote Airways was the obvious choice, and in October 1938 the new company was formed. Curly Evans, while continuing as a shareholder, stepped out of his active role in the airline as the growth of his own trucking business demanded more of his time.

CF-AUX, now sporting the new company logo emblazoned within a

flag painted on the aircraft's door, was
spending a lot of time flying into
Zeballos, on the west coast of
Vancouver Island. A gold strike was
raising a fever of activity, and Ginger
was quick to open a base at Zeballos to
compete with the CPR steamer
Maquinna, which was providing the
only freight and passenger service into
what was fast becoming a boomtown.
Ginger set up a scheduled air service
between Vancouver, Port Alberni and
Zeballos. Port Alice was later added to
the stops as that town's newly constructed pulp mill became another
source of business for the airline. It
seemed that nothing could stop the
growth of this popular airman's business as industry boomed on Canada's
west coast.

In the summer of 1938, Ginger
received a visit from another pilot of
renown, one Grant McConachie, who
was on his own road to fame as an
aviation pioneer. Like Ginger, Grant
also was a charmer, but one with far
greater entrepreneurial skills than
Coote. Word had it that McConachie
had sweet-talked his way into the heart
of a well-heeled European princess
who had helped finance his airline,
United Air Transport Ltd., based in
Edmonton, Alberta. UAT, as it was
called, had landed a lucrative mail
contract servicing Whitehorse, Yukon,

from Edmonton, with stops in British
Columbia. It was those stops in B.C.
that had Grant McConachie stymied.
Under the new regulations applicable
to his licence, McConachie could not
operate in B.C.—he needed to acquire
an operating B.C. airline, and who but
Ginger Coote could provide him with
just what he needed?

Lacking the nose for business of his
former partner, "Curly" Evans, Ginger
may have fallen in with McConachie's

Two of Ginger's Fairchilds share Zeballos harbour with Gordon Ballantine's Bellanca Pacemaker. Pilots paddled out to the moored aircraft in a dugout canoe. ELWOOD WHITE PHOTO

22

plans much too quickly. The charms that had convinced the princess to provide a $54,000 Ford Trimotor to McConachie were no less effective when focused on this seasoned B.C. bush pilot. A new airline was formed, Yukon Southern Air Transport, of which Ginger and McConachie were shareholders. This gave McConachie what he needed and made Ginger a vice-president of United Air Transport. It was also the structure McConachie needed to create the airline that would one day become Canada's second-largest carrier, Canadian Pacific Airlines.

Earlier, pilot Russ Baker had bid Ginger farewell, moving sideways to the Canadian Airways Ltd. payroll. The well-known pilot then started up his own operation, which he called B.C. Central Airways. This airline would, in time, become Pacific Western Airlines (PWA). In the chain of takeovers and mergers so typical of aviation history in Canada, Russ Baker's PWA would, one day, own everybody—including what we are now viewing as the beginning of McConachie's empire.

Ginger replaced Russ Baker with Bill

Holland and one of McConachie's pilots, Len Waagen—the most experienced pilots on the coast. Ginger Coote Airways was, at this date, a force to be reckoned with. Then, on May 27, 1938, the company's flawless safety record took a hit. Len Waagen, with three passengers, went missing out of Zeballos while flying AUX on a scheduled flight to Port Alberni. That grim news was headlines for some months as a huge air search was mounted for the aircraft. As no sign of the familiar old Fairchild turned up, the papers moved on to other exciting aviation developments.

On August 4 of that year, Ginger, Grant McConachie and Grant's chief pilot, Sheldon Luck, made aviation history when they initiated the mail flight north to Whitehorse out of Vancouver. Using two aircraft, a Norseman and the new Fleet Freighter, and stopping at every major airport en route, the three popular airmen established an airline route that remains important today.

A year after the loss of AUX, a survey crew working out of the Franklin River area, near Port Alberni, heard the "ping" of raindrops on metal as they sat on a log, eating their lunch. Investigating this sound, unnatural in a forest, they discovered the wreck of the missing AUX with its grisly cargo.

It was determined that Waagen had slammed into the tall timber while manoeuvring in the fog-shrouded Alberni Canal.

Ginger's flying exploits continued to make the front pages of B.C. newspapers. He went on to save a few more trappers and prospectors, but the impetus of his airline's growth had served Grant McConachie's larger plan with the creation of Yukon Southern Air Transport, which carried on with the mail contracts and provided passenger service northward as far as Whitehorse. Ginger, the B.C. folk hero, was left with a handful of useless stock certificates in the now-defunct United Air Transport. He operated Ginger Coote Airways into the early months of the Second World War, at which time he sold the airline to his erstwhile competitor, Canadian Airways, and relinquished all his connections with it. The newspapers announced that their hero's plans were somewhat indefinite.

On October 12, 1940, what was to be the last pre-war photo of Ginger Coote to appear in the Vancouver papers was captioned "In Uniform Again." The accompanying article stated that R.L. "Ginger" Coote, pioneer B.C. flyer, had joined the staff of No. 9 Observers' School at Edmonton, as a pilot flying RCAF

23

24

trainee navigators on simulated bombing missions.

The name of Ginger Coote disappeared from the pages of B.C.'s newspapers. News of his once highly touted exploits was replaced by coverage of the larger events of the Second World War. While the airplane remained in the centre of attention for the newspaper reading public, it was featured not in the saving but rather in the taking of lives. A generation of young men was learning to fly, and the public imagination was no longer captured by the remarkable achievements of one pioneer.

The observer-trainees at No. 9 Edmonton were undoubtedly impressed with the piloting skills of this

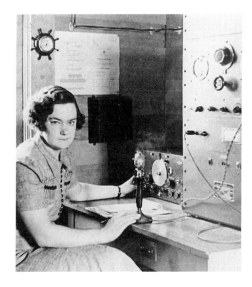

veteran bush pilot, but it was an ignominious end for a man who had pioneered the commercial use of aircraft in British Columbia. Ginger's business partners and employees had gone on to become recognized leaders in Canadian aviation while he contented himself with the cold morning task of starting an Avro Anson in Edmonton's frigid winter weather. Further indignity has been bestowed on Ginger by history itself in the all-too-rare mention of his great contribution to British Columbia's aviation legacy.

On January 14, 1970, the photo of Ginger published in many B.C. newspapers appeared under the headline "Funeral Set for Famed Pioneer Aviator." It was a picture the youngsters of the 1930s could relate to: Ginger wearing his fedora hat. Under its wide brim, Ginger Coote was wearing something else, something for which he would long be remembered: his famous and irrepressible grin.

Pioneer airman Russell (Ginger) Coote dies

Russel L. (Ginger) Coote, 72, a pioneer of commercial aviation in BC and a legend in his own lifetime, has died after a long illness. A private funeral will be held today in Chilliwack.

Mr. Coote established airline routes into the Yukon and to the west coast of Vancouver Island but won fame for his many mercy flights into remote areas of BC in the 1930s.

His only navigational aids were oil company road maps and a flying instinct that he referred to as his "dead reckoning."

Born in Chilliwack, he was the son of distinguished BC pioneer Lieut.-Col. Andrew L. Coote who settled in the upper Fraser Valley in 1890 and was a leader in community, civic and militia affairs.

Young Coote joined the Westminster Regiment as a bugler at the age of 12.

Three years later, at the outbreak of the First World War, he transferred to the 47th Battalion, CEF, and went to France as a sniper and scout. He was the best shot in his regiment.

At the age of 17 he won his commission and was wounded twice at Vimy Ridge. After recovering in England, he transferred to the Royal Flying Corps and began a way of life he was never able to leave.

After a brief career as an oil company agent and a try at farming in the Fraser Valley, he acquired a Detroit Eaglerock aircraft and went barnstorming at county fairs in the Cariboo.

By the start of the 1930s he was flying the twin to Lindbergh's Spirit of St. Louis and had established a flying school at Chilliwack.

One of his first co-pilots was the late Russ Baker who became another bush pilot and airline founder.

Mr. Coote got into the airline business by following the gold strikes to Bridge River, Wells and Zeballos.

It was during these years that, between flying men and equipment to the mines, he became famous for his mercy flights.

By 1940 it was estimated that Coote had saved more lives than had been lost in aviation in BC.

From the beginning, he maintained that flying was the safest means of travel and he survived one crash and several forced landings without injury.

Once, when forced down in the Straits of Georgia, he paddled his monoplane seven miles to Point Grey where he was able to get a tow from a passing fish boat.

By 1938, Mr. Coote was flying the mail from Ashcroft to Fort St. John and was building up an airline to Whitehorse that later was to be taken over by the late Grant McConachie of Canadian Pacific Airlines.

He made many trips into the vast areas of the Stikine and Omineca to pick up injured trappers, lost hunters and the sick.

Later, in 1938, the business had been renamed Ginger Coote Airways and regular flights were made to Zeballos and other isolated areas on the west coast of Vancouver Island. It was later bought by the Gibson Brothers who were then logging at Tahsis.

Ginger Coote's great love was for the Cariboo, it's people and the fishing and he continued to fly charter flights into the area until eight years ago.

He said his favourite pastime was flying airline pilots into remote lakes on fishing trips without any navigational aids.

He flew "by the seat of his pants," to the very end.

FAMILY: His wife Molly; a daughter, Mrs. Jocelyn Parsons; one grandson, and a brother, Colonel Ian Coote in England.

25

2

THE SHORT, FURIOUS HISTORY OF PIONEER AIRWAYS

Many of British Columbia's early coastal airlines were founded on a wing and a prayer and a pilot's innate desire to fly—but not this one. Pioneer Airways had it all: top pilots, the best aircraft, lots of passengers and, most important, a bank account! How did such a well-founded airline slip so quickly into obscurity—to be denied even a small mention in the pages of aviation history?

Bill McCluskey was standing on the cabin-top of the little flying boat. He was waiting to jump to the dock as the craft came alongside. It was cold as hell in Ocean Falls on this day, and he would have to take care not to slip on those frosty planks. Well practised at his job, he made the leap without incident, taking a quick turn of the aircraft's rope around the dock's tie-up rail all in one fluid movement. The aircraft snugged up to the dock as McCluskey blew into his hands and looked around.

Commanding the scene was a massive concrete spillway sloping upwards some 700 feet from the inlet to Link Lake, a small body of water atop the surrounding hill. The lake's water was at this moment coursing through giant penstocks, down the spillway into a concrete structure at the bottom. McCluskey's aircraft, a Boeing C204 flying boat, had just descended from the lake above, paralleling that spillway in its controlled descent onto the choppy waters of Cousins Inlet. The pilot had viewed this scene a hundred or more times and was not conscious of the pervasive hum made by the hydroelectric turbines that robbed the energy from the descend-

28

ing lake water. He had flown many types of airplanes into Ocean Falls over the years, and for a variety of little coastal airlines, none of whom were now in business.

As he stood there on the dock, looking up at the townsite, McCluskey would have seen the giant paper mill dominating the northeastern end of the Inlet—a man-made scar on a magnificent natural wilderness. In this year of 1935, the Pacific Mills Co.'s paper mill at Ocean Falls was a major player in the province's economy, which was now, slowly, recovering from a dismal economic depression.

For McCluskey, this was a place where a pilot's dreams were made. He was going to start his own airline right here in Ocean Falls, and Pacific Mills, who also owned the town, were as good as partners in the project. The hundreds of company employees who lived in these brightly painted bungalows hanging onto that steep hillside would be his passengers, as would the Native people at nearby Bella Bella and the employees down-inlet at Namu, where B.C. Packers' fish cannery was located.

This 38-year-old ex-military pilot was happy about a lot of things on this day. He was particularly proud of the brand-new airplane he was flying—the very best for the job. The Boeing C204

Thunderbird had been built right in downtown Vancouver at the Hoffar's boatyard in Coal Harbour. There had been just four of the model built so far, and it was a real winner. Soundly constructed of laminated spruce with fabric-covered wings, this double-wing flying boat was strong, fast enough in the air and quick out of the water. The Pratt & Whitney Wasp engine developed 410 horsepower and had proven to be very reliable in many aircraft types over the years. It was pedestal-mounted on the 204—mounted between the wings in the "pusher" configuration. This radial engine would push the plane, its pilot and four passengers along at 95 miles an hour. Not the quickest plane in the world, thought McCluskey, but the plane had a good range from the fuel in two wing tanks. These tanks each held 32 gallons, and the special tank he had installed in the fuselage, aft, carried an additional 35 gallons for long trips up the coast.

There weren't many pilots around with McCluskey's experience, and unlike those many little airlines that kept going out of business after a few weeks, his airline would survive with that big captive market available to him. Such were the thoughts that made pilot-entrepreneur Bill McCluskey a happy man on this day.

Through the enthusiastic efforts of Pacific Mills' accountant, Bobbie Roberts, subscriptions supporting the airline totaled $13,000—no small sum in January 1935, when the airline was established.

"William R. McCluskey, you've got it made," he said to himself, and laughed.

"Hey McCluskey, what are you grinning about?" The voice came from one of the company papermakers, Bobbie Roberts, as he made his way down the ramp to the seaplane dock.

"I was just admiring the new name," McCluskey grinned, standing aside and theatrically gesturing to the large, bold letters flowing from the plane's bow. They read, "Pioneer Airways Ltd.," and under this name appeared the port of registration: "Ocean Falls, B.C."

"It's downright magnificent," Roberts observed, as he joined the pilot in admiring the plane. "Is it really ours?" he asked.

"Your friend and mine, Mister Hunter Wells, signed her over to us as of this sunshiny morning," laughed McCluskey, as he passed an official-looking document to his friend. "That's what you get in exchange for your $4,000," he added.

"Me and all the others," Bobby chuckled.

The two men were referring to the fact that their new company of Pioneer Airways was incorporated with a group of subscribers made up of ten equal shareholders, five of whom were papermakers with Pacific Mills. Papermakers were very well paid; they were key men in the mill's operation and were influential with both management and the employees. Also among those original subscribers were two millwrights and a local logging contractor—the airline had every angle covered and, not surprisingly, was popular among local residents.

The Pioneer Airways concept resulted from the footwork of Bobbie Roberts, who also performed as the paper mill's accountant. He had ramrodded the sale of shares in the new company, knowing it was a sure thing if everyone supported the project. He knew from experience that the many long, rainy days experienced in this inlet drove people bananas, and sooner or later everyone would use the airline to get out of town. Having a famous coastal pilot like McCluskey was the ace in the hole. Roberts had everybody in Ocean Falls excited about owning their own airline and having it based right here in this rainy inlet.

"We're going to need another airplane," McCluskey said as they walked up the ramp, making for the hotel.

"Before we turn a wheel, he wants two planes!" Bobbie laughed. "But I know what you're saying."

"Yeah, when I'm away on a long flight and somebody needs a plane out of here, we're up you-know-where

29

without a paddle. I've got a friend flying for Ginger—Bill Holland—he'll come with us. We'll get another 204."

As the two men walked up the icy street they were met by the mill manager, Frank Drumb. Drumb had heard the plane come in and had slipped out of the office to view the aircraft, which was now drawing the attention of a small crowd of locals. Like the other key people at Pacific Mills, Drumb owned a share in the new airline.

The directors of the little company met that night in the Martin Inn, the company-owned hotel, and voted in favour of purchasing another Thunderbird flying boat. McCluskey knew that Boeing had a brand-new one, built in 1931, which had never been assembled. Arrangements were made to have Boeing's agent, Hunter Wells, acquire the craft and have it put together at Wells Air Harbour at Marpole on the Fraser River. It would be delivered to Pioneer Airways ready to fly. McCluskey was further instructed to hire Bill Holland as the second pilot. Pioneer Airways was taking shape: two aircraft, CF-ALC and CF-ALD, two pilots, ten shareholders and a bank balance of $9,000 generated from share subscriptions.

It was January 22, 1935, when that meeting took place at Ocean Falls. The newspapers made no mention of Pioneer Airways, but on that same day, down in Vancouver, the province's premier, Duff Pattullo, announced the certification of the bridge across the Fraser River that would bear his name. Across the country, in Ontario, that province's premier, Mitch Hepburn, was reported to be reorganizing relief plans for the thousands of unemployed people who needed food and shelter. There was also a report in the papers that in Geneva, Switzerland, the governments of Great Britain and France were in agreement concerning peace overtures to be extended to Italy for the next day's session of the League of Nations. On that January day in 1935 it looked like the world, including Pioneer Airways, was on course to a brighter future.

William R. McCluskey, a former fighter pilot who had been awarded the Distinguished Flying Cross during the recent war, was a highly experienced and well-liked coastal pilot. He was a married man and a practising Catholic with six children. He and his family had recently relocated from his hometown in Vernon, B.C., to what he called the Big Smoke—Vancouver. When he took off out of Ocean Falls the next morning he was bearing a new title: general manager and chief pilot of a new and

well-founded airline. McCluskey dropped three passengers at Powell River before proceeding on to Vancouver, where the B.C. registrar of companies officially recorded and validated the incorporation of Pioneer Airways. The registered office of the company was shown in that document to be Room 603 in the Vancouver Block, 736 Granville Street, Vancouver—the office of the company lawyer, David McKenzie.

The airline now entered into business and, as predicted, became very busy performing daily scheduled service between Ocean Falls, Powell River and Vancouver. Charter flights were conducted as far north as Prince Rupert, and almost immediately the airline was awarded the mail contract for its three principal ports of call.

After the delivery of Pioneer's second aircraft, Bill Holland came on strength as the second-string pilot. He too was good press for Pioneer, as he had a long and enviable flying record throughout Canada and was well thought of all along the B.C. coast. The word was out among companies and individuals who chartered airplanes that Pioneer, with its Thunderbirds and high-time pilots, were safe and reliable—the best air service to deal with in British Columbia.

The two pilots shared the flying in both the scheduled flights and the growing number of charters. When business permitted, they would each take some time off, remaining on call in the event that the duty pilot became swamped with bookings. By July of that year, only seven months after start-up, Pioneer Airways was a going concern.

On Saturday, July 27 Bill McCluskey began a typically busy week. He took off out of Ocean Falls in ALD and flew to Prince Rupert, where he picked up passengers and proceeded north to Stewart. Returning to Prince Rupert with an additional load, the pilot made it back to Ocean Falls on Sunday and on the Monday morning carried passengers down to Alert Bay. He returned to Ocean Falls late in the afternoon, and there he loaded the flying boat with passengers: Paul Armour of the Armour Salvage Co., Bobbie Roberts, on airline business, Reid McLennan, the government returning officer, and William Faulkner, Pioneer's aircraft engineer. They took off and before nightfall made it as far as Alert Bay, where they spent the night in the Nimpkish Hotel. A very early departure at 5:45 the next morning had the aircraft arriving at Wells Air Harbour in Vancouver at 8 A.M. McCluskey was beat—he went home

to bed while engineer Faulkner drained the oil, checked the filters and refilled the crankcase with Castrol 90 before going home to bed.

Sometime that morning, a booking was made to fly a party of three up to Gun Lake, in the Bridge River country. Bill Holland was out flying, so McCluskey was called in to perform the charter in ALD. He arrived in time to depart the river at 2:30 P.M. with two passengers, R. Brock, dean of applied science of the University of British Columbia, and David Sloan, the managing director of Pioneer Mines Ltd., in the Bridge River community of Bralorne. Dean Brock advised McCluskey that he wished to stop at Alta Lake, along the way, where they were to pick up Mrs. Brock before proceeding to Gun Lake. It was explained that Mrs. Brock was spending a holiday with her two sons at the family summer home, near the present village of Whistler.

The trip to Alta Lake would have taken less than an hour in the C204, but it was nearly 4:30 P.M. before the pilot and his three passengers returned from visiting the Brock summer home to the Alta Lake dock in order to continue their journey up to Gun Lake.

Bill McCluskey taxied the flying boat off the dock in the late afternoon's hard, gusting winds. The pilot had

carefully warmed up the engine prior to casting off, and when clear of the dock he taxied back half a mile, then turned into wind and opened the throttle on the Wasp to full takeoff power. The aircraft lifted off the water and climbed, slowly, on a south heading, toward the rising and heavily timbered shore. It was reported to have not gained more than 125 feet of altitude during this initial climb-out before banking steeply to the right to avoid the fast-approaching trees. The flying boat was seen to slip in the turn, then plunge into a clearing on the northeastern shore of the lake. The impact of the crash broke the aircraft's back, and the pedestal-mounted engine "pendulumed" forward, smashing into the cabin and killing pilot McCluskey and his front-seat passenger, Dean Brock, instantly. The occupants of the back seat, Mrs. Brock and David Sloan, were gravely injured. Sloan would survive, but Mrs. Brock died while being transported, in a speedboat, to hospital.

In Geneva, the appeal to Italy to abandon her claim to Abyssinia was unsuccessful. In Ontario, the newly funded soup kitchens were helpful to some, but many still went hungry. In Vancouver, Premier Pattullo's bridge was forgotten as a pall of shock fell over the community with the report of

UBC dean R.W. Brock (left) and his wife (centre) died in the crash of Pioneer Airways flying boat CF-ALD, as did pilot Bill McCluskey. David Sloan (right), a Pioneer Mines Ltd. executive, was seriously injured but survived the crash. Brock was a high-profile B.C. resident who was deeply mourned in military and educational circles in the province. Mrs. Brock died en route from Squamish to Vancouver by speedboat.

34

this tragic death of the most eminent engineer, scholar, humanitarian, soldier and educator in the province. The sad circumstances of Mrs. Brock's death, following that of her famous husband, added to the calamity, and B.C. newspapers carried letters of tribute for many days thereafter.

Seemingly forgotten in accounts of the history of B.C. aviation, Pioneer Airways and its famous pilot, Bill McCluskey, joined the legion of failed coastal air services.

Postscript
Company records show that Hunter Wells was paid in full for both airplanes, one of which now lay in a

crumpled heap by Alta Lake; a lake judged by pilots of all eras to be a dangerous choice. However, at that time, roads did not serve the more suitable choice, Green Lake, three miles away.

It became a question among aviators of that day as to why McCluskey had not taxied all the way back to the southern shore before attempting the takeoff. The 16mm movies taken of the accident by Dean Brock's son are not now available to prove or disprove the theory that had he not precipitated the takeoff, the accident would not have occurred.

In May 1936, the shareholders of Pioneer Airways attempted to breathe

William R. McCluskey learned to fly with the Royal Flying Corps and served in the First World War with distinction. His performance on the day of the accident may well have been the result of fatigue from his long hours of flying during the previous days. A 16mm film made of the takeoff by R.W. Brock's son proved that he did not taxi back to the lakeshore. Pilots wondered why McCluskey did not use all of the lake available to him on that fateful afternoon; the prevailing wind on Alta Lake is known to create gusting conditions.

new life into the company by going public, but the attempt failed to gain that public's interest.

CF-ALC, the remaining flying boat, was sold to Tommy Jones, who operated an aircraft maintenance shop at Wells Air Harbour. Somehow, the aircraft got badly bent and was sold off for parts.

Brock Hall stands on the University of British Columbia campus as a lasting tribute to the former dean of that university's Faculty of Applied Science.

Bill Holland added to his fame by performing feats of great skill and courage while flying military aircraft to Britain when he was engaged with Ferry Command during the Second World War. He returned to civil aviation in 1945. His life ended in a Lockheed 14 somewhere in the Coast Range of British Columbia.

Ocean Falls changed hands, over the years, from Pacific Mills to Alaska Pine and Cellulose and then to Crown Zellerbach. It was finally shut down, and the buildings and equipment were auctioned off.

Only ghosts occupy what is left of the townsite that could once boast that it owned its own airline.

Acknowledgement
Bobbie Roberts's son, Vern, who is now retired from the forest industry, supplied much of the information and all the photos for this article.

35

JOURNEY LOG: — JUNE 15, 1939

Putting your life in someone else's hands was an everyday occurrence for the aircraft engineers who flew along with the early bush pilots. Cecil Pickell lived to tell his tale; many did not.

It used to be that pilots were accompanied on their flights by a qualified aircraft engineer. These necessarily ingenious men travelled with a well-stocked tool kit and many aircraft and engine parts deemed essential for the aircraft's continued operation. The mechanics could also anticipate being used as helpers for the plane's many loadings and unloadings on its supply runs for customers and the restocking of fuel caches.

The flying was usually done in support of a survey or mining exploration team. It required the pilot and engineer to set up a bush camp beside a river or on a lakeshore near the operation. In this bush camp they would attempt to maintain some comfort despite harsh weather, mosquitoes, black flies and meals that were considerably less than gourmet fare.

Such was the role of Cecil Pickell in the summer of 1939, when in the employ of Grant McConachie's and Ginger Coote's newly amalgamated airline, Yukon Southern Air Transport. Cecil was based at Dease Lake with pilot Charlie Tweed, maintaining a famous Fairchild FC-71 bearing the registration CF-ARM.

"Close by, at a little place called Boulder Lake, they were having a mini gold rush," Cecil recalled. "We were performing a contract to haul supplies in for the miners and had our fuel cache at Dease Lake. It was our habit to replenish our fuel by flying in drums of gas from Juneau, Alaska."

One day in 1939, a miner showed up with tons of gear to fly in to the mine. Since

Previous page:
Pictured is a
Fairchild 71 similar
to that flown by
pilot, Charlie
Tweed, on that ill-
fated morning. The
pilot had no forward
visibility during the
extended take-off
run in his heavily
loaded aircraft.
When finally "on
the step" Tweed's
view through the
morning fog was
further obstructed
by the engine
cylinders.

their fuel supply was dangerously low, the two aviators decided to fly into Juneau during the evening, load the plane, then take off first thing in the morning to restock their fuel cache before starting the big freight haul. They did this on the evening of June 14.

"The next morning, when we taxied out into the bay for takeoff at Juneau, the plane felt very heavy. She was drawing a lot of water from the weight of the fuel drums aboard," Pickell explained. "Charlie Tweed figured she'd take a long run to get up on the step before becoming airborne," he added, explaining that this wasn't unusual in this type of flying in those days.

"That old Fairchild had zero visibility forward over the engine until she got up on the step, and even then the most you saw was cylinders and spark plugs," Cecil explained, as he went on to describe the fact that Juneau harbour narrows at the mouth. "There are three big wooden dolphins driven into the sand bars to warn deep-sea ships of the shallows," he explained. "These posts are the same colour as the beach, and on this morning they were absolutely invisible. We were taking off toward the narrowing gut of the harbour, and when we finally got up on the step those three dolphins were right there in front of us—we hit them square in the middle at full power, just seconds before liftoff."

The narrator was obviously shaken even now, many years after the event, as he recalled that tragic morning. "The impact from the collision split the engine in half and tore both floats apart—one on either side of the dolphins. The prop was bent double over what was left of the cowling, and the aircraft burst into flames immediately."

Cecil had been thrown onto the floor of the plane by the impact and was reaching over toward the pilot to see if he was okay when, suddenly, everything went black. "The last thing I remember," he recalled, "was getting a hold on Charlie's sleeve. Then the fuel load blew up and I went through the roof."

Miraculously, Cecil Pickell survived his journey through the fuselage roof of the aircraft from the power of that blast. He landed in, and was immediately revived by, the glacial waters of Juneau harbour. "Two little kids, paddling around in a canoe, saw it all and paddled up as close as they could get to me. The flames were said to be roaring 200 feet into the air," he said. "I had to battle my way clear of the burning water to reach those kids."

The two boys attempted to pull Cecil aboard their craft but were frightened by his condition—naked, burned, hairless and blackened with a huge, bleeding gash in his arm. They held on to him and waited for help, which was on the way from a passing motor launch. "The launch was run by a Captain Smalley, who got me on board and rushed me to the local hospital. There was nothing left of the Fairchild, and poor Charlie was gone," Cecil recalled.

Cecil Pickell had a crushed hip, a broken arm, a huge gash on the other arm, a mangled foot and substantial burns. The doctors told him he would never walk again, but he would prove them wrong—though the man suffered much pain from these injuries throughout his remaining life.

"A funny thing happened following the accident." Cecil was telling me this 55 years after the event, so he could afford a wry smile in recollection. His boss, Grant McConachie, asked him at his hospital bed if he and Charlie had been drinking that day.

"Hell, no. What gave you that idea?" Cecil replied indignantly, to which McConachie stated that the doctors had said that Cecil was full of booze.

"I couldn't figure that one out until later, when Captain Smalley came by to see me. He explained that when they got me out of the water I was shivering so badly that he gave me a shot of Scotch." That shot of Scotch turned into another one and another, until he had consumed the entire bottle before being admitted to the hospital.

Cecil Pickell was 74 years old when he told me this story. He was then living at Charlie Lake, a famous aviation place near Fort St. James, B.C. His son maintained the family's aviation tradition by owning an aircraft and operating it for his construction business. The aircraft was kept at the family's private airstrip.

We know that Cecil flew with his son in that aircraft, and he may even have helped to repair it from time to time. But we don't know if he ever had another drop to drink.

3

THE PRESS AND PADDY BURKE

In which is related an old story of the first and arguably the greatest air search in British Columbia's history, told with the assistance of the newspaper articles of the day and with some astonishing insights from a participant in the search, pioneer aviator Ted Cressy.

There was once a mystique about the newspaper business and a matching romanticism about piloting airplanes. In the 1930s, many people were convinced that newspaper reporters always wore a fedora hat, just like celebrity radio columnist Walter Winchell. Aviators could be identified by helmet and goggles, as worn by "Lucky Lindy" in his 1927 solo flight across the Atlantic Ocean. In addition, reporters were considered brash and aggressive, typing their "scoop" with the two-finger hunt-and-peck system while talking with a cigarette constantly wagging in their mouth. Pilots, on the other hand, were squinty-eyed hero types, handsome, clever and devil-may-care. It was a

"made in Hollywood" concept perpetrated by films starring city editor James Cagney and "cub" reporter Mickey Rooney or, for aviation, Hell Diver pilot Clark Gable and his co-pilot, William Bendix, doing snap-rolls over the heroine's house with a good-luck teddy bear stuck atop the instrument panel.

Hollywood notwithstanding, this myth was in place for readers of the *Vancouver Daily Province* and the *Vancouver Sun* newspapers on October 20, 1930, when each reported that a well-known British Columbia aviator had failed to show up on a flight from Atlin, B.C., to a place called Liard Post. Both newspapers carried a short column on an inside page, and neither of them knew that the helmet and goggles and the fedora hat were about to become equal participants in the biggest air search and biggest reporting marathon in the history of British Columbia. In the typical pyramid style of news writing, the following column appeared in both papers:

THE VANCOUVER DAILY PROVINCE, October 20, 1930

AVIATOR MISSING AGAIN

Capt. E.J.A. Burke, aviator, is again missing somewhere in the Liard River District.

Capt. Burke took off from Atlin a week ago for a Hudson's Bay post on the Liard River. He was supposed to be back in two days but has not been heard from for nearly a week.

It is thought that Capt. Burke has been held down by the cold snap. His plane is equipped with floats and has not yet been changed over to skis. The weather was fairly mild when he took off from here with plenty of open water on the lakes. A sharp frost set in after he left and it is possible the lake or river on which he landed froze over during the night.

Word is being waited by Air Land Manufacturing Co. here, by whom Capt. Burke is employed, as to weather conditions in the north before organizing a search party. If winter has set in a ski equipped aircraft will have to be sent in.

Capt. Burke was forced down on a small lake in the same district in August by a shortage of gasoline and was marooned for ten days.

Previous page: Former air force squadron leader Paddy Burke (left) with his engineer, Emil Kading, and the infamous Junkers CF-AMX. This photograph was taken in Atlin, B.C., shortly before the tragic events of 1930.

PETER CORLEY-SMITH

COLLECTION

Newspapers were then the sole source of breaking news for an event, the failures and tragedies of which would guide the shape of air search and rescue in years to come. The press did not fail to play up the names of Paddy Burke's passengers on this fateful flight. "Three Finger" Bob Marten, a prospector, was a favourite (we never learned what happened to the other two fingers), and Paddy's aircraft engineer, Emil Kading, also was aboard CF-AMX, the single-engine Junkers Model C13 aircraft flown by the former air force squadron leader, Paddy Burke.

The next reported item appeared in the *Vancouver Sun* on October 25, when an itinerant pilot, located in Hazleton, volunteered to search for the overdue Junkers.

THE VANCOUVER SUN, October 25, 1930

SEARCH FLYER AT TELEGRAPH CREEK

Pilot Frank Dorbrandt, United States aviator, en route from Hazelton to Atlin to begin a search for Capt. E.J.A. Burke, Vancouver flier who with two companions has been missing in the Liard River district since Oct. 10, arrived here at 5 o'clock last evening following a hazardous trip.

It took Dorbrandt four hours and twenty minutes to complete his journey. A heavy snowstorm prevented him from making better time.

Frank Dorbrandt, who just happened to be available while flying from Seattle to Anchorage, found himself in some pretty sticky weather and was himself posted as missing when he failed to arrive at Atlin. However, he showed up at Telegraph Creek and resumed his search from there only to disappear again on his flight to Liard Post. Little concern was felt for Dorbrandt because he was considered a very experienced northern flyer, and sure enough, he landed at Cassiar short of fuel. He reported that he had made it to Liard Post and provided some important news to the searchers—Burke had made it to Liard Post and had left there to return to Atlin on October 11.

Dorbrandt fades from the scene at this point, flying on to his destination at Anchorage. But he had established Burke's last known position. This information narrowed the search area considerably. Dorbrandt's report, which was received on October 30, also established that Burke and his party had now been missing for 19 days and that no search had been initiated.

Meanwhile, in Vancouver, a new and important player arrived on the scene—a man described as a veteran pilot for Alaska–Washington Airways, one Robin "Pat" Renahan. With his engineer, Frank Hatcher, and a mining prospector named Sam Clerf, Renahan took off from Vancouver on October

27, bound for Atlin to join the search. He was flying a Lockheed Vega on floats and was carrying a set of wheels for the plane, which he planned to use when the lakes froze up solid. Sam Clerf was a friend of Paddy Burke and had been Burke's companion in an earlier incident, when the two had been stranded in the bush for ten days after their aircraft had run out of gas. Renahan figured Clerf was a good man to have along, because he knew the area so well. The *Daily Province* reported the story on October 27:

44

THE VANCOUVER DAILY PROVINCE, October 27, 1930

PAT RENAHAN HOPS TODAY FOR ATLIN

Special Fast Plane to Be Used in Rescue Work

Pat Renahan, veteran pilot for Alaska–Washington Airways, accompanied by Frank Hatcher, air engineer, will hop off from Vancouver at noon today to take part in the search for Capt. E.J.A. Burke, aviator, missing in the Liard River district of the lower Yukon for the past 17 days.

Burke left Atlin October 10 accompanied by "Three Finger" Bob Marten, a prospector, and Emil Kading, an air engineer, to visit a prospect of Marten's near Liard Post. They have not been reported since and are thought to have been caught by a sudden cold snap and frozen in at one of the small lakes in the district.

Burke's plane had not been switched over to winter landing gear and was equipped with pontoons.

Pat Renahan flew to Seattle this morning, where he picked up a Lockheed Vega seaplane which was especially tuned up for him at his company's Seattle hangars, He has received permission from R. Carter Guest, District Inspector of Civil Aviation for BC and the Yukon, to use the American-registered ship during the search for Burke.

The Lockheed has a top speed of 160 m.p.h., and Renahan expects to make Ketchikan or Juneau tonight. He prefers using a pontoon-equipped ship rather than wheels at this period of the year for work in the north country.

There is a possibility that Burke may be out of gasoline on a lake that has frozen over. Renahan can land successfully on the ice with pontoons if necessary. Should the ice prove too thin to hold the weight of the ship the pontoons will float it.

Inclement weather delayed Renahan, but he did leave Vancouver on Tuesday, October 28. He was reported at Alert Bay on the way to his first stop at Swanson Bay, where a radio station was located. The station was closed for the season, but fuel was available there for Renahan's continuing flight to Prince Rupert. No further word was received from Renahan, so it was presumed that he was holding at Swanson Bay. Weather conditions along the coast were typical for the area at this time of year, and since the aircraft was not radio-equipped, it was not unusual to lose track of it from time to time.

The plot was definitely thickening when, on November 4, the *Province* ran the following article:

SEARCH FOR RENAHAN TO START TODAY

Last Sighted at Butedale
May Have Damaged Plane in Landing at Dusk on Tuesday

Definite word that Pat Renahan, Vancouver pilot who left here on Tuesday to join the search for Capt. E.J.A. Burke in northern British Columbia, reached Butedale and started for Prince Rupert has been received by the Canadian Fishing Company.

Renahan has been unreported for four days, and a relief plane piloted by Ansel Eckmann, senior pilot for Alaska-Washington Airways, will leave Seattle early Sunday morning to make a search of Lowe Inlet, Ogden Channel and other waters north of Butedale.

Andy Johnston of the Canadian Fishing Co. at Butedale reported that Renahan and his two companions, Frank Hatcher, mechanic, and Sam Clerf, prospector, landed at the cannery to refuel shortly before 5 P.M. Tuesday and left at 5:20 P.M. The pilot expressed the intention of reaching Prince Rupert before dark, declaring that he could do the 100 miles in three quarters of an hour.

Visibility Was Poor, Gale Blowing

The visibility was poor at the time and there was a strong southeast wind blowing. Darkness set in at 6:15 so that Renahan had a narrow margin in his attempt to reach Prince Rupert before nightfall.

Under these circumstances, fears for Renahan's safety have increased and the Seattle relief plane will make all possible speed toward the northern waters where he may have experienced trouble.

The weather along the northern coast has been overcast during the past two days but flying was possible and it is thought that if he were delayed by fog in some isolated bay he would have had one or two chances to get off. It is feared that in making a landing at dusk on Tuesday Renahan's plane was damaged and he has been unable to proceed.

Renahan left Vancouver at 12:15 noon on Tuesday and was thus well on schedule when he reached Butedale.

Burke was lost for more than a month before an official search was launched.

BRIAN BURKE PHOTO

The search for Burke took on new dimensions when Ansel Eckman failed to locate Renahan's aircraft during his sweep up Grenville Channel to Prince Rupert. Two aircraft were now missing. The press revealed that a fisherman had spotted Renahan's Lockheed Vega, flying low in the dark, at the north end of Grenville Channel at 6 P.M. the previous evening. That aircraft had never arrived at its destination of Prince Rupert.

Faced with this turn of events, the U.S. Navy launched two aircraft from San Diego to join the search for the missing Americans. These aircraft also ran afoul of weather and never made it to the scene. The Royal Canadian Air Force, caught sitting on its hands until now, was shamed into action by the U.S. Navy's offer of assistance and sent two aircraft to help search for Renahan. No RCAF aircraft were ever employed in the search for Burke—it seems he was just a Canadian.

The local press stated that the search had become more of a "campaign," with only private interests involved in seeking the fate of what had now become a search for six missing men. Alarmed at the obvious confusion, Mrs. Burke, wife of the missing Paddy Burke, sent the following telegram to the *Vancouver Sun* on November 7.

Mrs. Burke's letter was published in the *Sun*, and it seems to have lit a fire under the Vancouver aviators, who formed a search organization. They got together at the Boeing plant in Vancouver to plan strategy. The meeting was presided over by Henry Hoffar, president of Boeing's Vancouver operation. The group determined that the Burke party had now been missing for 27 days and the Renahan search party had been missing for 10 days. Although there was search activity for Renahan, the Burke search had stopped dead and something had to be done. The group appointed pilot W.A. "Bill" Joerss to take charge of search operations out of Atlin. Joerss was directed to depart immediately for Atlin.

Flying in a sister ship to the missing Junkers, Joerss left the next day in company with pilot R.L. Van Der Byl and engineer Ted Cressy. The *Sun* reported an interesting side story to the event:

THE VANCOUVER SUN

FORMER FOES OF AIR FLY TOGETHER

Errands of Mercy to North Heals Old Enmity

One of the stranger coincidences of life was noted in the recent flight from Vancouver of the Junkers seaplane CF-ALX on its attempted errand of mercy to the north in the fact that two former enemy war pilots, R.L. Van Der Byl and W.A. Joerss, fought in the air on opposite sides during the European conflict. T.H. Cressy, air engineer on the flight, also served with the Royal Flying Corps during the war.

Joerss was an excellent pilot, experienced in the very country in which the search was being conducted, but his pilot's licence had been suspended for some minor infraction of air regulations. He was, therefore, unable to fly. Now placed in charge of the search operation out of Atlin, he appointed Van Der Byl as his pilot and Ted Cressy as engineer in a flight to Atlin via the inland route to Prince George. Two other aircraft provided by Pacific International Airlines also made that journey north. It was planned that these three aircraft, in company with the Treadwell Yukon Co.'s Bellanca, would perform a systematic search of the area. Treadwell's aircraft, already back on the search, was flown by pilot E.L. Wasson, a young man who was soon to make a name for himself.

If it wasn't enough that two airplanes were now missing, the two search planes accompanying Joerss on the flight out of Vancouver crashed along the way. No one was hurt in this bizarre turn of events, but now these aircraft were out of commission too. Readers of Vancouver's three daily newspapers were getting the idea that flying in northern British Columbia was like booking a deck chair on the *Titanic*.

At Prince Rupert, the search for Renahan's Lockheed was drawing a blank despite the arrival of two Loening flying boats from the U.S. Navy and the two Fairchilds from the RCAF. A body had been spotted floating in the waters of the Portland Canal, but extensive searching failed to recover it.

Reporters were having a field day with the events. Each issue of the newspapers revealed new clues in the search for Renahan, and many columns were dedicated to interviews with family members of the missing men. In particular, Renahan's young wife captured the sympathy of readers when it was revealed that she was not only the mother of an infant son but was also pregnant with her pilot-husband's second child. The distraught woman had set up a vigil at the Vancouver airport, where she stayed, encouraging the searchers. But all hope for her husband's survival was dashed when a set of wheels, identified as cargo carried aboard Renahan's Vega seaplane, were washed up onto the shore.

The search for Paddy Burke, which had turned into the search for Pat Renahan, was about to become a comedy of errors, when the *Province* ran the following news item:

THE VANCOUVER DAILY PROVINCE

ANOTHER AIRPLANE MISSING

3 Vancouver Men in Burke Search Unreported

Still another missing plane is added to the two already lost in the north. The Junkers seaplane CF-ALX piloted by R.I. Van Der Byl and carrying W.A. Joerss and Ted Cressy, who left Vancouver Sunday to take part in the search for Capt. Burke.

The Junkers, CF-ALX, was last reported leaving Prince George for the next leg of its northern hop on Tuesday. At the latest, it should have reached Atlin Wednesday afternoon, but it is unreported.

Out of Touch

After leaving Prince George the party would be out of touch with Vancouver until they reached Atlin, as they traveled far to the east of the telegraph line by way of Takis, Thutade and Dease Lakes. There is a possibility the plane has been frozen in one of those northern lakes.

The press nearly got it right that time: ALX had landed on Thutade Lake and had frozen in overnight. The three men had freed the aircraft from the ice, but the available takeoff area had been greatly reduced by the freeze-up, making takeoff with a full load out of the question. The three men had decided that Joerss was the more skillful pilot to get the craft airborne in the short run available. Van Der Byl and Cressy stood on the shore and watched Joerss successfully gun the airplane out of that short lake and make for Burns Lake as they had planned. Those left behind could expect a ski plane to rescue them; failing that, they hoped to enlist the local residents for help in obtaining a dog team for a long mush to civilization.

When Joerss landed ALX at Burns Lake, all hell broke loose for the unsuspecting aviator. He was almost clapped in irons for piloting an airplane while under suspension for having, earlier, flown an aircraft over its gross weight. To make matters worse, he was cited as a coward for having abandoned his friends in the wild at Thutade Lake. Nothing he said would persuade either the officials or the public that he had acted in concert with the decisions of his two companions. Ottawa took the only action it ever made in the entire search when the Department of Transport permanently suspended Joerss's pilot's licence. It would seem that Joerss was paying the price for having fought his war on the wrong side of the lines.

At this point, the press realized that the reading public might be confused with the sheer number of players in this fast-unfolding saga. Furthermore, the types of aircraft and their similar identifying registrations were enough to baffle even the most astute reader: AMX was Burke's plane—now lost for 27 days. ALX was the sister ship to Burke's aircraft, which was now joining the search but, seemingly, becoming lost itself. This aircraft, originally piloted out of Vancouver by Van Der Byl, had now suddenly showed up in Burns Lake with Joerss at the controls—Joerss, whose licence was under suspension and who had left his buddies, Cressy and Van Der Byl, at Thutade Lake. Then, of course, there was Renahan, with his passengers, Hatcher and Cerf, who were missing somewhere near Prince Rupert in a Lockheed Vega. Each of the Vancouver papers now ran photos of the people involved and an abbreviated recap of the events as they awaited breaking news on what was now a search for three airplanes with a total of nine people aboard.

That breaking news didn't happen, and an information blackout took place between November 21 and 24. During this time, an armada of aircraft were searching for the American, Renahan, while only one aircraft was searching for Burke—that one was flown by the young Everett Wasson, who was, ironically, an American flying a Bellanca owned by the U.S. mining company, Treadwell Yukon Co.

If this were a Hollywood movie, it would now flash back to Thutade Lake, where our two heroes, concerned about the long wait for a ski-equipped rescue plane, had decided to mush the 180 miles to safety. They hoped Joerss had made it to Burns Lake—but, if he had, why was there no rescue plane? Little did they realize that Joerss was being treated like a prisoner of war, his explanations and demands ignored.

Suddenly, on November 24, a long-awaited headline appeared in both newspapers:

THE VANCOUVER SUN, November 24, 1930

BURKE PARTY BELIEVED SAFE; LOST PLANE FOUND

It was Wasson, of course. The young pilot's methodical searching for the

past month suddenly paid off—there below him was the Junkers, AMX, frozen into the headwaters of the Liard River. Unable to land beside the plane,

Wasson flew back to Whitehorse to get help. He planned to land on a lake some 15 miles from the lost aircraft and walk in to the crash site. Wisely, he obtained the services of an experienced woodsman. He and a trapper by name of Joe Walsh flew in the next morning and mushed on snowshoes to the long-missing aircraft. There, they found a note carved into a tree: *"Left for Wolf Lake Oct. 17—want food badly."* — *Paddy, Bob, Emil.*

On December 5, the *Vancouver Province* ran the following column, explaining the exciting discovery and the action of pilot Wasson:

Missing Pilot and Companions Short of Food Seven Weeks Ago

LEFT TO HIKE TO WOLF LAKE

Search Flyer Fails to Find Sign of Trio on Trip Over Mountains.

Everett Wasson

Whitehorse Y.T. Dec. 5 — "We could find no sign of the missing men between the upper Liard and Wolf Lake," declared pilot E.L. Wasson on his return here Thursday afternoon with guide Joe Walsh to the headwaters of the Liard River to examine Capt. Burke's abandoned plane.

"We found the plane undamaged," he said. "There was no written note in the machine but inscribed on a tree at their camp fifty yards away was the message: "Left for wolf lake Oct 17—want food badly." It was signed by the three men.

"We landed at an Indian camp down river from the Burke plane and the Indians reported that Burke had flown over the camp looking for a landing place, but the lake was frozen solid at the time."

Everett Wasson, 24-year-old hero of the Paddy Burke saga, continued his search in the Treadwell Yukon Bellanca, visiting several Indian villages and the Wolf Lake site of Burke's fuel cache, but to no avail. The Burke party could not be found, but the young pilot, with Joe Walsh, was determined to locate the missing men. Well provisioned for a long stay in the bush, the two men flew and mushed until December 10th—almost three months since the Junkers went missing.

BURKE DEAD; TWO SAVED

Flier Finds Party 40 Miles from Spot Where Plane Crashed

Rigors of Two-Month Trek Out Too Much for Vancouver Airman: Death Several Days Ago Told

Whitehorse Dec. 10— E.J.A. Burke, aviator, who with two companions has been missing for six weeks in Northern B.C., has died of exposure some days ago, it was reported by Everett Wasson, who returned here today, bringing Emil Kading and Bob Marten, who survived the ordeal in the bush since the crash of their plane.

The missing party was found forty miles up river from where the plane was located.

Emil Kading, Robert Marten, Joe Walsh, and E. Wasson

Paddy Burke died from exposure after six weeks in the bush. It was rumoured that the pilot also suffered from diabetes, which added to his distress. His two passengers, engineer Emil Kading and prospector Bob Marten, survived the long wait for help.

52

They found Paddy Burke's body, watched over by his two emaciated companions, 40 miles up the Liard River from the ice-locked plane. At one time these men had gone 23 days without food.

The dramatic story started to unfold from the cracked lips of Emil Kading and Bob Marten. Burke had died on November 20, and after his death the engineer and prospector decided to stop hiking. They made camp using their sleeping bags on the open ground. Twice, Wasson's Bellanca had flown over them, but he did not see

their feeble waves and they had no beacon fire. The two men mustered their last pitiful strength and gathered wood to build a fire, should the plane return. It did, on December 10; they fired their beacon, and Wasson spotted the smoke immediately. He waggled his wings to assure them he had spotted them and then flew to a good landing spot 10 miles from the camp.

Despite the approaching dark and a fierce blizzard, Wasson and Walsh mushed to the survivors. They missed the camp in the storm. The next morning, the two rescuers searched for the men, calling out as they hiked. Their yells were heard by Marten and Kading, who desperately fired off their last round of ammunition, directing the searchers to their camp. That night the two survivors went to sleep with a full stomach and the assurance that they would see their homes once more. Sadly, this was not the case for their pilot and companion, Paddy Burke.

At his home in Atlin, among the photographs, newspaper clippings and mementos of this tragic event, Brian Burke, Paddy Burke's son, has the very tree trunk on which his father carved that desperate message of urgency 73 years ago, a poignant plea for help still calling out across the years:

"Left for Wolf Lake Fri-17th Oct. — Want Food Badly" — *Paddy, Bob, Emil.*

Postscript

The search for Paddy Burke and CF-AMX was now over, but the press continued to bring in reports of the continuing search for Pat Renahan and his two companions. Although their bodies were never found, the cabin section of Renahan's Lockheed Vega was, much later, dragged from the cold waters off Prince Rupert. It was concluded that Renahan had misjudged the time of nightfall and found himself flying, not only in heavy rain and very low visibility, but also with the added hazard of darkness—perfect conditions, unfortunately, for the tragedy of impacting the water at flying speed.

Ted Cressy and R. Van Der Byl, who were left at Thutade Lake when they elected to have Bill Joerss fly the Junkers out to Burns Lake, successfully mushed 180 miles in deep snow and freezing conditions. It took them a month to reach Fort St. James, a time during which they were thought to be lost. Strangely, no search was ever mounted for them—it seems that search and rescue was an unfamiliar term in those days. Their story, a compelling adventure, is told in detail in the following chapter. Ted Cressy lived in excellent health to the age of 94 and provided much of the information recorded here.

Bill Joerss, who left his companions, Van Der Byl and Cressy, at Thutade Lake, was vindicated by them and praised for his skill at getting the Junkers out of the frozen lake. Despite everything these two men said in Joerss's favour, the authorities were unrelenting and would not reinstate his flying licence. Joerss became a longshoreman and lost his eyesight in a bizarre accident for which there was no compensation. He returned to Germany in the care of a daughter and died before the Second World War.

Soon after I wrote an account of this tragic story in *Aviator Magazine* (April 1993), a letter arrived at the magazine's office. It was a very short letter, but certainly the most poignant I have ever received:

"Thank you for telling us what happened. Our mother never gave us the information about the death of our father, Pat Renahan."

The letter bore two signatures, one of which was that of the infant son who had accompanied Mrs. Renahan during her long vigil at the Vancouver airport. The other signature was that of the not-yet-born child she was carrying during those tragic days.

All photos and newspaper text courtesy of R. Carter Guest collection.

The newspaper clippings used in this story are accurate in text content to the 1930 articles. However, they have been redesigned to fit this book's format.

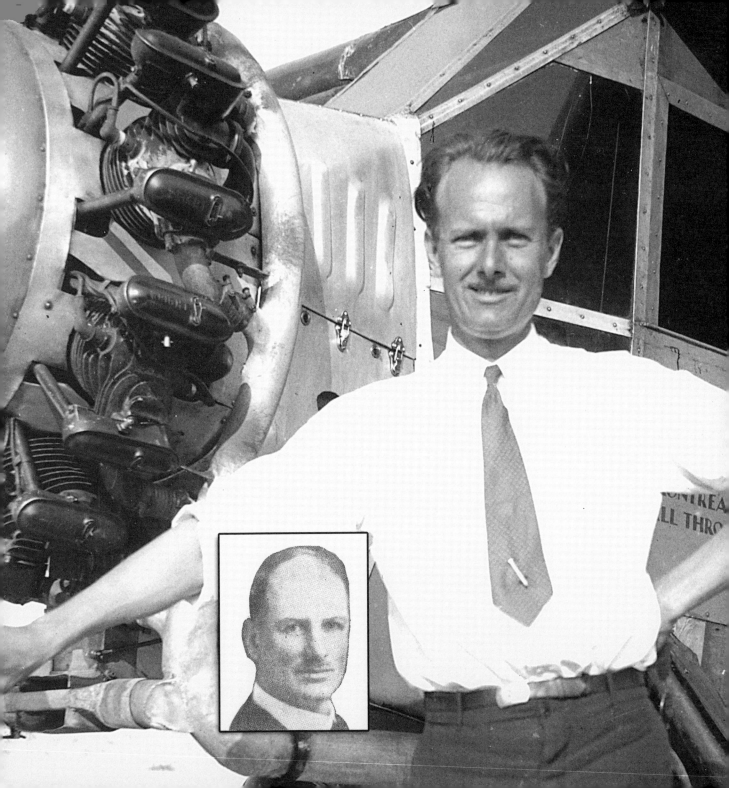

4

THE GREAT MUSH

Courage and determination were the personal attributes that saved the lives of two aviators abandoned in the wilderness of northern British Columbia in the 1930s. "We were never really frightened during the trek," said one of the survivors. "But we were grumpy as hell and arguing with each other every painful step of the way."

"A drama within a drama" was what Ted Cressy called it. He was referring to his and Bob Van Der Byl's adventures when they were left at Thutade Lake during the search for Paddy Burke's missing Junkers seaplane.

"We landed at 'Two Daddy Lake' around three in the afternoon," explained Cressy, who was recalling the details of his 1930 adventure, now 63 years later. "We had planned to make it to Summit Lake, but the weather turned really bad. A blinding snowstorm forced us to land sooner than we had planned."

Cressy, Van Der Byl and another pilot, Bill Joerss, were flying a Junkers C-13, CF-ALX, a sister ship to the missing aircraft. The three would-be rescuers had departed Vancouver on a mission to set up a search operation for the Paddy Burke party lost in the Liard River area for the past 27 days. The snowstorm that forced them to land at Thutade lasted all night and the temperature plunged. When Ted attempted to start the Junkers in the morning, it wouldn't respond and resisted all attempts for the next four days, during which time the ice built up in the middle of the lake.

"When we finally got the engine started, the spray from the prop froze solid onto the struts and pontoons. We must have added a half ton of ice to the airplane's weight," Cressy recalled.

Since Joerss was the more experienced pilot and knew the area well, the three aviators decided that he should fly the ice-heavy ship out of the lake and back to Burns Lake. From there, Joerss could arrange to send a ski-equipped rescue plane for his two partners.

Previous page: Ted Cressy, with his companion R. Van Der Byl (inset), mushed 180 miles on snowshoes over breaking snow after their unsuccessful attempt to join the search for Paddy Burke's missing aircraft. Cressy was an outstanding personality in the history of B.C. aviation, figuring largely in the early development of the industry.

"His takeoff was a classic," stated Cressy, recalling that Joerss carefully taxied the Junkers down the ice-free channel the men had recently cleared with a raft. Gunning the engine to full power, Joerss jumped the ship out of the water onto the solid ice in the middle of the lake and took off. "His technique minimized the amount of spray and ice build-up on the aircraft."

The veteran engineer became angry as he explained that Joerss was not supposed to be flying because he was under a licence suspension for having flown an overloaded airplane: "How do you load a seaplane, out in the bush, and know, to the pound, your gross weight?" muttered Cressy, revealing in his recollections that he was still indignant over the injustice dealt out to his friend so many years ago. "When Joerss showed up at Burns Lake, they nailed him to the cross and gave him a permanent suspension." "They wouldn't listen to him and accused him of abandoning us."

The two men had no way of knowing whether Joerss would make it or not and were concerned for his safety as they watched him fly into an approaching snowstorm. "We waited for sixteen days in the little cabin we had located on the lake. One night, two men burst into the cabin, pointing rifles at us. These were the owners of the cabin," explained Cressy. "Fortunately, they knew Bill Joerss. We kept yelling his name, and were eventually able to talk our way out of getting shot," he grinned.

The owners of the cabin told the two stranded aviators of an Native encampment at the end of the lake. The two men trekked there and made arrangements with a man by the name of Monassis, who agreed to guide them to the Bear Lake reserve. "Monassis was

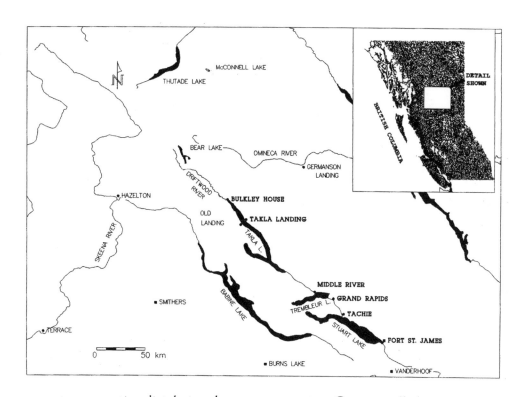

Facing page: Forced down by snowstorms, the three-man Burke search team became frozen-in on Thutade Lake. Skillful flying by Wilhelm Joerss got the ice-laden craft off the lake (note the ice buildup on the aircraft and the partially frozen lake). But Joerss had to leave his two companions behind to await rescue. He was treated very badly by authorities and wrongly accused of cowardice—and as a result, the rescue never happened.
TED CRESSY PHOTO, PETER CORLEY-SMITH COLLECTION

The map at right shows Thutade Lake district and the distance the two men mushed to Fort St. James.

a great conversationalist during that trek," laughed Cressy. "His sentences were five words maximum, but he was a helluva shot with his rifle—we ate Ptarmigan and Grouse when we ate at all."

The next 32 days were rough going. There was no crust on the snow, and their snowshoes broke through. Monassis led them over ridges and into valleys, taking short-cuts every so often. "We were totally committed to him by this time because we didn't have a clue where we were." On one occasion, Cressy recalled camping next to a big tree with a blaze on it. On the blaze were the names of seven Swedish miners who had disappeared several years earlier, when there had been some murders in this country. A Native by name of Gun-a-Noot had become the object of a police manhunt. "It was a little unnerving sleeping there, wondering if Gun-a-Noot had changed his name to Monassis," laughed Cressy.

The trio made it in to Takla Lake, where they were met by another Native, Thomesse Baptiste, who

THE GREAT MUSH

provided a dugout canoe. "We said good-bye to Monassis and boarded the canoe, paddling along the edge of the lake, where it remained unfrozen. We came down the Takla River, through Middle River and across Trembleur Lake. We then shot the grand rapids of Tachie, passing through the Tachie reserve, then paddled across Stuart Lake and arrived at McCorkell's store—that's at Fort St. James—around half past eight that evening—a fair day's travel."

Cressy and Van Der Byl had been trekking for 36 days, never getting out of the clothes they had worn since leaving Vancouver. "We were pretty ripe," laughed Cressy. "We located a motel of sorts, showered and changed our clothes and, as we were promised a meal by the owner, we sat down at the table and waited. The service didn't happen for a long time because the lady who owned the motel was also the local reporter for the Vancouver newspapers—she was off letting everybody know we had arrived."

Ted Cressy's wife was obviously very concerned over her husband's disappearance, and hope had been all but abandoned at this time. There was actually a plan to hold a memorial service for the two aviators when the two men finally showed up at Fort St. James. "My wife had been taken to a film showing by a neighbour on the day we showed up," remembered Cressy. "She was sitting in the Loew Movie House on Granville at Dunsmuir Street in Vancouver when a notice was flashed on the screen telling her to come to the office—she had liked that movie, but the news was better," laughed Cressy, recollecting her excited greetings.

The two men, who had started their trek on October 20, finally completed it December 23, 1930.

Postscript
Ted Cressy was a bear for punishment. He went back into the Liard River

country with Emil Kading and Bill Joerss to retrieve Paddy Burke's Junkers, CF-AMX. The damaged floats were removed and replaced with skis. The wings were taken off and the fuselage was motored under its own power to a frozen lake nearby, where it was reassembled and flown out. However, fate intervened and the BMW engine in the aircraft swallowed a valve. A forced landing was made at Bulkley House, where the aircraft was abandoned until the next spring.

Cressy and pilot Bill McCluskey returned the next year equipped with a brand-new set of floats, still in the crates, received direct from the manufacturer in Germany. When these were unpacked to install on the Junkers aircraft, the float fittings were found to be a mismatch. Cressy built a raft and floated the aircraft down the Takla River into Middle River and then across Trembleur Lake—his old stamping grounds from his 180-mile trek the previous year.

AMX was flown out, on wheels, from a field adjacent to the Hudson's Bay post at Fort St. James. Before taking off, McCluskey was warned by Ted Cressy to select the fuel onto the "Both On" position because Ted had determined that the fuel pump selector lever was "acting funny." McCluskey didn't do that, and he paid the price—

another forced landing, at Boston Bar into a strip cut into the side of a hill alongside the CPR tracks. On landing, McCluskey had to swerve to avoid some cattle on the strip. The aircraft slid backwards, down the bank onto the tracks.

This beleaguered aircraft, the object of the most extensive air search in the history of British Columbia, a central factor in the death of four men, reluctant to the end to give up the wilderness, arrived in Vancouver ignominiously strapped onto a rail car.

AMX was rebuilt in Vancouver and performed for many years with Pacific Airways Ltd. In the summer of 1938, the Junkers fulfilled its final destiny by carrying the pilot and two passengers to their deaths on a remote lake north of Fort St. John, where what is left of it remains to this day.

In telling me this story at the age of 94, Ted Cressy was bemoaning the fact that he had just had his driver's licence suspended. He would now have to walk; he thought that was a big joke. Ted Cressy passed away in 1995.

59

5

THE WHISTLING WHAT?

Pilots sometimes assign names to airplanes. "The Bat" was a racy little low-wing monoplane with the obvious registration of CF-BAT. "The Hummer" was another obvious derivative from the licence identifier, in this case CF-HUM, but this nickname was also appropriate because the plane had been converted from noisy piston engines to quiet turbines. Later, when registrations were issued with four letters, the two Mallards C-GIRL and C-GENT were referred to as "The Two Washrooms." "The Whistling Shithouse" was perhaps the rudest name assigned to an aircraft, but it was not meant to be derogatory—it was, in fact, a veiled tribute to a great airplane.

First of all, the name—Stranraer—was a challenge. Seemingly nobody in the press could spell the name of this airplane correctly, and that "r" in the middle also created a hang-up for correct pronunciation. The Earl of Stranraer, for whom this 1935-designed flying boat was named, likely had the same problem with his mail, as did the town named after him, which was located on Britain's west coast.

Those who flew the airplane would call it a "Stranny," or sometimes, as a joke, "the Strainer." This latter name referred to the maze of flying wires and interplane struts connecting the upper and lower wings. The wind created during flight was "strained" through these wires and caused the aircraft to whistle softly. Yes, it was a biplane and yes, the wings were rag-wings, whereas the fuselage was of riveted aluminum skin, formed into a quite graceful flying boat hull. The body swept up dramatically at the tail and sported two rudders mounted atop a large horizontal stabilizer with matching "singalong" wires and struts.

All of this assembly was pulled through the air at a maximum speed of

90 miles per hour by two Bristol Pegasus radial engines swinging massive three-bladed props. It was a very ship-shape airplane with stainless-steel hull fittings; rope cleats and rope lockers were accessible through a round sliding hatch cover in the nose or, rather, the bow of the craft. This aircraft, which whistled and appeared to be a throwback to the dawn of flight, was to become very famous on Canada's west coast.

William Mitchell, the man who designed the Spitfire, created the Supermarine Stranraer in 1935 for the Royal Air Force. The RAF needed an airplane to perform anti-submarine and reconnaissance work, for which the Stranraer's slow speed and long range made it admirably suited. The design was then given to Canadian Vickers Co. of Montreal to manufacture the Canadian version. Now the Royal Canadian Air Force could also be equipped with this maritime aircraft for the protection of both coasts.

Twenty of these aircraft served in this reconnaissance capacity during the early stages of the Second World War, but they were soon replaced with more suitable bombers, which escorted the shipping convoys from Canada's east coast to Britain. On the west coast, the Stranraer remained in service for a little longer before being replaced by the PBY or Consolidated Canso flying boats. Many Stranraers went into storage during the war and were sold off by the War Assets Disposal Corp. at the end of hostilities. In 1946, four of them were purchased by Jim Spilsbury's Vancouver-based Queen Charlotte Airlines, and therein hangs this tale.

Spilsbury & Hepburn Ltd. was a Vancouver-based communication company that operated a single-engine Waco seaplane to provide mobile radio service to fishing boats and coastal ships working the B.C. coast. The company pilot, Johnny Hatch, complained that he was being continually propositioned to provide transportation for the fishermen and loggers working the many camps that were springing up along the coast. Hatch suggested to company owner Jim Spilsbury that they might do better by providing flying services than by fixing radios. This was in 1945, when industry was getting back into gear after five years of war. The long-established coastal steamship service provided by the Union Steamship Company was reliable but very slow, and men and industry were now impatient to speed up the transportation into the B.C. hinterland.

Pilot Hatch, undoubtedly carried a few passengers back and forth during

"Over my dead body!" exclaimed the DOT inspector when he heard that Jim Spilsbury was planning to use retired RCAF Supermarine Stranraers for coastal passenger service. But Spilsbury and the "Stranny" prevailed, and the unlikely aircraft provided yeoman service for a decade. The Stranraers flew in the livery of two successive airlines— Queen Charlotte Airlines and Pacific Western Airlines.
ROY MOULTON PHOTO

this time and likely charged them for the service. This amounted to what the industry called "chisel chartering"—the illegal use of private aircraft to fly for hire or reward. The civil aviation authorities were ever on the alert to enforce the rules, so Jim Spilsbury quickly applied for a licence to operate a coastal air service. He would name his airline after the Queen Charlotte Islands, which he surmised would be the furthermost destination for his airplanes.

In these immediate post-war years a body of political appointees called the Canadian Transport Commission (CTC) ruled on the approval of airline licensing. Their mandate seemed to be that nobody could do anything until

they, the CTC, had sat on it for at least a year. Further, they had a nice, tight ship consisting of themselves, Trans-Canada Air Lines (now Air Canada), the Ministry of Transport (MOT, soon to become DOT) and the Canadian Pacific Railway (CPR). The last-mentioned had reluctantly been permitted to form its own airline under tight restrictions on the level of service allowed. The CTC's main job was to protect Trans-Canada Air Lines, the public airline, from any competition. Anyone believing that they could break into this little club was in for a tough ride. So, where did this guy Spilsbury think he was going?

In Jim Spilsbury's personal account of what he later called "The Accidental

Facing page: Many humorous stories surround the Stranraer flying boat. Pilots loved the craft and were quick to defend its stable flight characteristics. The most-told tale is that of the crew member who, from the forward rope locker, held up a sign that told a U.S. Navy jet that was flying alongside, taking pictures, to F– – – Off.

Airline," an engaging story emerges. Spilsbury's principal adversary and detractor, Canadian Pacific Airlines (CPA), was operating a few aircraft on the coast and resented the intrusion of another carrier. It was invited, by the CTC, to oppose Spilsbury's application. The big rail/air company prepared a legal brief for the court hearing—and an office clerk accidentally mailed it to Jim Spilsbury instead of the CPR's legal department in Vancouver! When the hearing took place, Spilsbury's newly formed Queen Charlotte Airlines (QCA) won the day, hands down, while the CPR company lawyers were rendered speechless without a prepared presentation. That CPA brief had somehow fallen into Spilsbury's garbage can.

If the sudden emergence of the upstart QCA wasn't a bad enough shock for the establishment, they were now faced with the Stranraer being the company's aircraft of choice. "Over my dead body!" sounded Carter Guest, the MOT inspector for British Columbia, who envisioned maintenance and corrosion problems with that old bird. One might be inclined to favour Mr. Guest's apprehensions when viewing this unwieldy-looking craft, considering the many advances made during the wartime development of aircraft: the Stranny appeared to be a throw-

back to the early 1930s.

Yet, despite being a rag-wing biplane with flying wires and struts, the aircraft proved itself time and again as an excellent choice. In its service to the coastal float camps and marine communities, the Stranny earned the affections of passengers and crews alike. For some 18 years it plied the skies between Vancouver, the mid-coast area and Prince Rupert. The Stranny, ever at 90 miles per hour, became famous.

When QCA took delivery of the four ex-RCAF Strannies, each airplane came equipped with regulation relief tubes, which allowed their wartime male crews to urinate overboard during the 12-hour patrols. The relief system was basic—a rubber hose through the hull which vented just below the craft's water line. On the inboard end, the hose was fitted with a small rubber funnel; there was a hook on the hull, on which this device was hung when not in use. An RCAF placard warned that the tube must not be left off the hook when the aircraft was on the water because the system would then work in reverse and the sea would leak into the plane. Spilsbury decided to leave this system intact and ordered a shower curtain to be installed around the seat at which the relief tube was located.

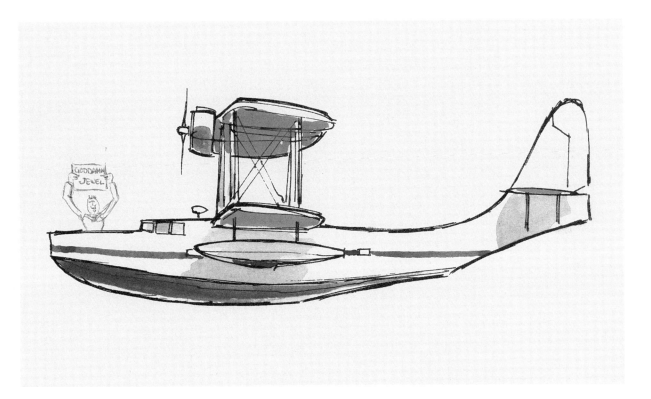

Since the shortest flight of the Stranny was a four-hour journey from Vancouver up to Sullivan Bay, the relief tube became a popular amenity, and much humour resulted from its use by the 20 passengers carried in the plane. Considerable speculation arose as to how the women passengers managed with this male-designed apparatus. It became a common topic of conversation during the long, cold and draughty trips up and down the coast. The relief tube also gave rise to a new name for the venerable flying boat. The Stranraer was now christened "The Whistling Shithouse" by one of its pilots. The never-ending joke came to an end, however, when a passenger failed to hang up the tube on one of the Strannies and it filled with seawater over night. The unfortunate plane was found, the next morning, on the bottom of the harbour.

The Stranraers soldiered on for many years as QCA grew to become a highly regarded airline. The long trips

THE WHISTLING WHAT?

Flying in a heavy snowstorm, this Stranraer caught a wing tip while manoeuvring in tight quarters at the entrance to Allison Sound. All survived because of fast action from the nearby logging camp. The wreckage was visible for years, serving as a warning to other pilots. Then, one day, suddenly it was gone. The Canadian Museum of Flight in Langley, B.C., salvaged the aircraft and is rebuilding it for display. U. ISSEN PHOTO

66

were soon phased out in favour of DC-3 airliners on scheduled, instrument-guided flights between major points along the B.C. coast. Seaplanes integrated with regional wheel-plane service became the trademark of QCA as the airline prospered over the years.

Like many coastal airlines, QCA drew the attention of those who wanted to amalgamate several small services to form a regional carrier.

Singling out QCA as having the optimum route structure and the operational savvy, Russ Baker of B.C. Central Airways sought to take over the operation by fair means or foul. When he set in motion his plan for the takeover, he found his match in Jim Spilsbury and was ultimately forced to pay a tidy price. This amalgamation created a new company, Pacific Western Airlines (PWA), which while

So beloved was the Stranraer to those who flew it that Jim Lightbown bought CF-BXO when it was scrapped. A group of enthusiasts rebuilt the craft, planning to charter it out for freighting and sightseeing flights. Financial problems crashed the project and BXO ended up in a museum in London, England. Pictured is the unique takeoff method employed for the test flight of BXO, after its rebuilding was completed, at Abbotsford airport.

THE VANCOUVER SUN: Mon., June 11, 1962

—Don LeBlanc Photo

NOVEL TAKEOFF was made by this Stranraer flying boat piloted by veteran pilot Slim Knights at Abbotsford airport Saturday. Aircraft was mounted on dolly and when flying speed was attained lifted off successfully. Dolly rolled to stop at end of runway. Flying boat was flown to Fraser River at Sea Island. Stranraers were used by RCAF during the Second World War.

bidding for B.C. regional status ultimately became Alberta's provincial airline and grew into one of Canada's major domestic air carriers. In the course of its growth PWA surprised everyone by inhaling the huge Canadian Pacific Airlines and emerged into world-class service under the name of Canadian Airlines International.

Now integrated into Air Canada, the branch of the airline's family tree that flew an airplane known as "The Whistling Shithouse" seems quite obscure these days. But listen closely, and you might hear that inimitable whistle through the flying wires. And within the draughty cabin of this redoubtable boat, you might just hear the complaints of loggers and fishermen of old, muttering about freezing to death in this haywire old airplane—an airplane that "stops at every jerkwater joint on the B.C. coast and takes for-bloody-ever to get there."

Now, doesn't that sound familiar?

FLIGHTS OF FASHION

In the early days of flight, as commercial aviation increased, so did the public interest in airplanes and in those daring men who flew the rag-wing and tube biplanes. Hollywood was quick to cast a romantic glow on the subject of aviation and make heroes out of this new breed of macho man. Pilots were credited with a courage that had hitherto been the property of sea-going adventurers. Naturally, fashion quickly followed reality—or was it the reverse?

It all started when Orville (or was it Wilbur?) put his cap on backward. The glamour of flying airplanes was captured in that simple act, and for a decade thereafter airmen wore their caps backward—peak to stern, so to speak. Ladies swooned, for glamour must always have its audience. *Vogue* and *Vanity Fair* magazines depicted their skinny fashion models draped languorously around a lift strut of an early aircraft. In the background of these fashion photos, a pilot would have his cap on "lock." Soon, a pair of goggles was added to the ensemble and Mesdames were further entranced.

Fashion and glamour have, since then, been associated with flying. From the early success at Kitty Hawk, North Carolina, to the moon landing, Hollywood played no small part in creating the aura of bravura surrounding those who flew aeroplanes. It was the derring-do of the business that helped create the hero concept that defined early aviators, and their wardrobe became an integral part of the mystique.

Immediately following the First World War, aviators dressed for the practical consideration of warmth. Flying around the sky at about 120 miles per hour with the top half of your body exposed directly to the super-cooled slipstream and the other half only partially

70

protected by the open cockpit could get a bit coolish—particularly in northern climes. A long leather coat resembling the type then issued by the Russian KGB for their spies was worn by aviators of the day. Under this coat would be found the popular "Teddy Bear" suit. The pilot's head was protected with a down-padded leather helmet while goggles were worn to keep the eyeballs from freezing and to act as a personal windshield in the rain.

The constant spray of castor oil used in those early engines was repeatedly wiped off one's face with a white scarf worn rakishly to blow in the slipstream. No reference was made to the more obvious effects of an environment charged with castor oil. The pilot's hands were protected by fleece-lined gauntlets that had shields fanning up from the wrists to halfway up the arm. Mukluks or fleece-lined boots were also worn, and the entire ensemble was capped with a huge fleece collar. Nobody talked about the dress code for underwear. A friend of mine has saved his father's underwear, which was worn with all of the above while flying Curtis HS2Ls out of the Canadian Soo in 1920. While the wooden hull of the HS2L was thought to gain weight during the season by absorbing water into the wood, the truth is out—it was really the pilot's skivvies that altered the lift-drag ratio of that venerable aircraft.

In those days, the frame speed of movie cameras was eight frames per second, which gave the heavily garbed pilots an appearance of moving about swiftly in a jerky, animated fashion while flashing a lot of quick little smiles. When those old films were rerun at real speed, it was found that these men were in fact dragging themselves around with the weight of their gear. What had been considered to be smiles were in fact grimaces of discomfort, caused by wool-to-skin irritation from the long johns. Many quick little hand movements, missed in the early flics, showed up in the reruns but were edited out for the sake of propriety.

Helmet and goggles added a certain flair to the attire of early birdmen. The Gosport tubes connected to the earpiece were small, enema-type hoses, not to be confused with early aircrafts' pilot-relief tubes. Speech through either was quite unintelligible.

R. CARTER GUEST SCRAPBOOK.

De rigueur for serious aviators, circa 1930.

R. CARTER GUEST SCRAPBOOK

Hollywood could do little with this garb. The physical attributes of its leading men were lost in the folds of fleece. However, the emerging fashion of a quasi-military-looking leather jacket with riding breeks, white shirt, silk scarf and helmet with goggles was much more to the filmmakers' liking. Clark Gable soon appeared on the billboards wearing such a rig. That actor's inimitable curl of hair at the brow, his steely look as he gazed up at the gathering sky, set a standard that has plagued aviators to this day. It is claimed that the early airlines required pilot-candidates to have perfected at least one steely look. It also became a requirement that the captain be handsome and decisive while the co-pilot be an amiable bumbler with a big nose. Open any flight-deck door to check this out and you will find a Jimmy Durante in the right seat—the guy wrestling with the stewardess is the captain.

Other conventions established by Hollywood in the numerous flying movies produced in the 1930s dealt with Lady Luck. Pilots were heavily into sheer luck in those years. Flying by wire at that time referred to how the wings were attached, and many a thespian pilot plunged earthward with at least one wing flapping in the breeze because his luck simply ran out. The co-pilots were often depicted as having some sort of talisman that maintained luck on side so long as this empowered object was aboard the aircraft—a teddy bear or a horseshoe was a popular choice. Foreshadowing was achieved when Pooh Bear missed the flight or the horseshoe slid down a longeron and lodged, undetected, against the control column.

In one aerial epic, the rear cockpit co-pilot, played by William Bendix (he has the big nose), develops a predictable habit of sticking his chewing gum onto the aircraft's rudder before each flight. On one occasion, when he forgets to thus stabilize his Dentyne, we are given the distinct feeling that something dire is about to take place—I recall the

71

An early advertisement for what was referred to as the "Teddy Bear" flying suit. In extremely cold climates Mukluks were added.

audience exclaiming, "Oh, no!" If you missed the inference, the music comes up ominously as we cut to Bendix in the back cockpit, aghast that his Double Bubble is still in his mouth and not parked on the rudder. At this point, the horseshoe slides down the longeron and locks up the elevators. Clark Gable, up front practising his steely looks, can't pull the stick back and the craft starts into a power dive.

We cut from desperate Clark to the horrified, gum-chewing Bendix, then a cut to the aircraft in a vertical dive, then back to Clark, over to Bendix (swallows his gum) back to screaming plane. When the smoke clears, there is Clark, a smudge keeping company with that curl on his brow, kicking his toe into the smoking rubble of the aircraft. He reaches down and, sadly, retrieves— you guessed it—a smouldering teddy bear and two Double Bubble hockey cards. The high-booted, riding-breeked, white-scarfed and leather-jacketed Gable looks skyward as the film fades out with an ethereal vision of good old, big-nosed Bendix cracking his gum in the heavens.

Hollywood came on strong during the early 1940s with a rash of wartime flying movies featuring many of the same old stars but now wearing a brand-new wardrobe. Randolph Scott, Clark Gable, John Wayne, Gary Cooper,

Van Johnson and, you guessed it, William Bendix (still in the right chair) were now out of the breeks and high boots. They now favoured the U.S. Air Force fleece-lined bomber jacket and the resplendent uniforms of the Marine Corps and Naval Air Force. While helmet and goggles were still being worn by the fighter jocks, the bomber crews wore their regular military-issue peaked caps while flying. These caps became the subject of a fashion style during the Second World War. Originally supplied with a wire inside the crown to keep the cap in shape, it became cool to remove the wire so that the top of the cap became soft and floppy—better suited to the wearing of headphones. The fashion statement of the day was to make the cap look pretty tacky by kicking it around the drill square, running over it with a truck and generally beating it into the shape one would expect of a cap that had seen 32 missions over Berlin. Milton Caniff, an outstanding illustrator of the 1940s, devoted an entire Sunday page of his famous comic strip "Terry and the Pirates" to an explanation of this chapeau ritual.

Flight gear may have changed, but Hollywood found it hard to kick the "smouldering teddy bear syndrome," and early wartime movies were plagued with a similarity in plot to that of their

Hollywood's glamorous treatment of aviators in early flying movies created an aura of "derring-do" for pilots—a stigma that has prevailed to this day. The film makers also created a public attitude toward the safety of flying that took years for aviation to live down. The media continues to find flying accidents more interesting than the industry's great achievements.

"B grade" pre-war versions. Not so with J. Arthur Rank and other British filmmakers, who eclipsed Hollywood with authentic flying pictures. Tinseltown had to pull up its fleece-lined socks. It stopped hand-shaking mocked-up cockpits for the in-flight sequences and devoted some of the budget to air-to-air photography.

Paul Mantz, long the technical adviser and stunt pilot for Hollywood flying pictures, found himself working a little harder. Mantz was a holdout for the riding breeks and helmet, which, along with a twirly moustache, were his trademark. He soon bailed out of moviemaking and the void was filled by others who provided the know-how for some of the most exciting and realistic air-to-air photography thus filmed. Notable among the newcomers behind the aerial productions was Frank Tallman, who in later years performed the flying sequences for *Waldo Pepper* and the definitive Battle of Britain movie.

The British filmmakers didn't seem to care if the hero had a big nose or not, so Bill Bendix was belatedly given four bars to wear. But he never actually made it into the left seat of any movie. The jet age was upon us, and Bill Bendix's teddy bear failed the medical.

Since the dawn of aviation history, the pilot's wardrobe fit the needs of

the craft and carried with it an air of glamour that gave pilots the reputation of being irresistible to women. To determine if this remains the case in the age of Mach 2, I interviewed a jet pilot at the recent Abbotsford, B.C., air show. I caught this pilot, completely encapsulated in a G-suit and still wearing the helmet and smoked-glass facemask, descending the stairs of an F-18 fighter jet.

"Can we be frank?" I asked. "Does being a pilot get you into more sexual encounters?"

A muffled laugh issued from behind the inscrutable visor, and the disconnected oxygen line wagged like a dog's tail. Gloved hands reached up and removed the helmet. A riot of blonde hair fell from the casque and I was greeted with a dazzling smile.

"Not that I've noticed," she laughed.

HANGAR FLYING: FLIGHTS OF FASHION

6

THIS SYLVESTER WAS NO PUSSYCAT

The "romance of flight" is a somewhat poetic turn of phrase when applied to someone like William Beresford Sylvester. Bill would probably prefer the more homely diagnosis of having had "the flying bug" all his life. That "bug" brought him a life of high adventure, and along the way he founded what would become the largest seaplane operation in the world.

He was bored. There was an emptiness in his life that wouldn't go away. He had all the trappings of success, all the freedom and all the possessions he once envied of others—an expensive car, his own private seaplane, his house paid off, good cigars and fine clothes. The destitute Bill Sylvester of the past, cutting and delivering firewood, had been a happier man than the flush, well-groomed version that now looked out at him from the mirror.

It was the sense of enterprise that was missing. Bill had honed it to a fine edge during his early days in the U-Drive business and again, later, when he started B.C. Airlines. All that purpose was now missing from the life of William Beresford Sylvester. The nouveau riche Sylvester straightened his tie, checked his immaculate half-Wellingtons and donned a three-quarter-length car coat that gave him what he hoped was the appearance of a country squire. Lurking very close to the surface of this self-made man was the simple country boy who didn't reflect from the mirror but whom he recognized as his real self.

He had been a crack shot with a rifle, back in those beginning days—moving effortlessly through the bush without making a sound. Stalking a deer, he would silently manoeuvre himself downwind of the unsuspecting animal until the crucial moment. Then, one shot was all it took—the Sylvester family would eat tonight.

You might wonder how a boy growing up within a stone's throw of Victoria's staid Empress Hotel could develop such skills. It's a two-part answer: in 1920, the Empress was not that far from the forest; and in those days, Bill Sylvester had no choice—he had to be a good hunter or go hungry. His mother and his younger brother depended on him to put food on the table. Hunting wasn't a hobby for Bill—it was survival.

The rough times experienced by the Sylvester family during Bill's early school days were made even worse by the untimely death of his father. The family was left with little else but its home in the "Dardenelles" area—that, and a failing feed-store business located at the foot of Yates Street.

The family business may have been some help in young Sylvester's business training, but as soon as school was completed, Bill had to get out and earn a living very quickly. He turned to what he knew best—the bush. With the same dogged determination that had made him an effective hunter, he set out to drop trees and buck them into firewood for sale and delivery to the then 40,000 wood-burning residents of Victoria.

While building his fuel business, Sylvester kept his eye out for other work to augment his small income. His energetic activities were noticed by Bill Morrow, a prominent Victoria businessman with considerable property holdings in the growing capital city. Morrow judged Sylvester's potential correctly and put the energetic young man to work running a U-Drive operation in the business centre of the city. Bill ran his wood deliveries and the U-Drive simultaneously. Morris Kersey, an early friend of the young huckster, recalled how he did this: "In those days, U-Drive cars were rented in the evening. A young fellow could rent a car to take out his girl for about three dollars. Funny as it seems now, that was the main source of business. Very few rentals took place during the day, so Bill could do both jobs. Sylvester and I shared a room together at this time and I just never ever saw the man—he worked day and night."

An eccentric millionaire by the name of P.J. Hobson, who was backing some of Bill Morrow's enterprises, was responsible for Sylvester's first major business break. It seems that Morrow had become delinquent on payments to the millionaire while on one of his not-infrequent alcoholic binges. This indiscretion brought about the loss of his U-Drive business and its transfer to his wealthy creditor. The millionaire gave Sylvester an opportunity to buy the business on terms he couldn't refuse—nothing down, and payments of 20 percent of the take. The first thing the young entrepreneur did was to name the business after himself— Sylvester U-Drive.

During these early years Bill Sylvester married Dorothy Morrow, the daughter of his former employee. He also met three people who would figure large in his future: Bill Dunbar, who operated the Sussex Hotel for the Royal Trust Co. and who was a wealthy man in his own right; Eric Cox, Dunbar's accountant; and Stan Scurrah, a businessman who would ultimately manage Sylvester's operations. These men were thrust together from the circumstances of doing business in a small city; everybody knew everybody in Victoria during those days, and these three would continue as business partners for the rest of their lives.

In 1935, Bill Sylvester was doing well enough to become interested in learning to fly. He took lessons from Terry Finney's Flying School, operating out of Esquimalt harbour. The flying "bug" truly bit Sylvester, and he became an enthusiastic private pilot. Flying on floats, he could now practise his consummate hunting skills near the lakes and inlets of the B.C. coast. His enthusiasm led him to believe that his successful U-Drive business could

prosper even more with an airline affiliate. In 1939, he bought two Luscombe 8As as part of his plans to start his own airline. The international situation put a damper on these plans, and the aircraft went into storage for the five-year duration of the Second World War. "In storage" meant behind the Sylvester U-Drive building, which was located behind the Sussex Hotel. Those airplanes made this building a popular landmark in Victoria during the war years. On the days when Bill ran up the engines of the little planes, a crowd of people gathered around to witness the event.

Among Sylvester's personal traits were cleanliness and tidiness. He had a penchant for emptying ashtrays and sweeping floors—rarely was the man seen at the office without a polishing rag in his hand. During the early U-Drive days, having eight or more cars to clean and polish, Sylvester still had room for one more, as his friend Morris Kersey relates: "A man by the name of McDermott, known to all of us as "Mr. Mac," saw how shiny Bill kept his U-Drive vehicles so he had the energetic Sylvester polish and clean his brand-new Dusenberg every day. I don't know if Mr. Mac ever paid Bill for his troubles, but Sylvester didn't care about that—he just loved to keep that car in sparkling condition."

Such personal tics gave some people the idea that Sylvester was a bit of a joke. But they soon learned that he was not a man to trifle with. One who learned was a businessman by name of Hill.

Across the street from Sylvester U-Drive was the only competitor in town—Hill's Drive Yourself Cars Ltd., said the sign. Bill eyed that business with a fast-developing acquisitiveness. He figured there was only room for one U-Drive in town, and it was going to be Sylvester's. "The licence plates for the two competitors' cars were in numerical sequence to assist the police in recognizing the rental cars in town," explained George Williamson, whose brother worked for Sylvester during the war years. "Pretty soon all those numbers were Bill's—Hill's U-Drive was history. I don't know how he did it, but Sylvester was pretty proud to call himself 'Mr. U-Drive' in Victoria."

The former woodcutter was into natty, three-piece suits now, and the busy shipyards and wartime naval and military bases in Victoria were bringing prosperity to the rental-car business. There was now more to car rentals than taking your girl for a spin, and Bill Sylvester started to benefit from his previous long hours of hard work.

At home, though, Sylvester was in trouble. He was a proud father of a young son, but his marriage was on the rocks. "He just didn't spend enough time tending the home fires," explained his friends from those troubled days. The war clouds were now clearing, and Bill threw himself into his plans for his airline.

His application to the Department of Transport for an air charter licence brought forth an intervention from no less than Grant McConachie of Canadian Pacific Airlines. In the ensuing court hearing, McConachie insisted that CPA had more than enough aircraft to serve the needs of British Columbia. The judge, however, agreed with Sylvester and awarded the U-Drive operator a Class 4 charter licence, which resulted in the launch of B.C. Airlines. From the court proceedings Sylvester realized he was now playing in the big league and that the big players didn't like the idea of a hustler like him muddying the waters. The former woodcutter liked this kind of challenge and charged ahead with enthusiasm. "He hired me while I was still in the air force," laughed George Williamson, who started flying for Sylvester on a $50-a-month retainer. "And that didn't include the use of my 1941 Plymouth Club Coupe as the airline's office at Vancouver airport," he added.

There were no facilities for a flying school on the south side of Vancouver

George Williamson was hired by Sylvester at $50 per month while he was still serving in the RCAF. The new, underfunded airline operated from Williamson's car until the Vancouver airport built a shack for the flying school and seaplane charter operation. The one-room shack also housed Sylvester's principle competitor, Vancouver's U-Fly, resulting in many a hi-jinx as each company accused the other of stealing customers.

COURTESY GEORGE WILLIAMSON

Airport in 1945, and Sylvester's new business would have to fend for itself. This was also the case for a competitor in the business: Vancouver's U-Fly, which was also preparing for what was hoped to be a peacetime boom in flight training. The City of Vancouver, which then owned the airport, reluctantly dragged a small building into place for use by both companies. Although they were direct competitors, the two firms did business under each other's noses. Williamson recalled how difficult it was to keep business secrets in these close quarters: "Harry Swiggum, who flew for us in those days, used to count out the day's take in a loud voice, trying to get a rise out of the U-Fly people, located four feet away. Of course, he would add a few hundred dollars to the total, just to make it

sound good. U-Fly finally moved out and constructed their own building."

Bill Sylvester had started B.C. Airlines with the two Luscombes purchased before the war. He now purchased a Waco model ZKQC6 cabin biplane on floats. "That Waco weighed in at just 18 pounds shy of full allowable gross weight," Williamson laughed. "But I recall flying it on its first charter flight with an 1,800-pound load. It was a bit slow off the water on that trip." The Waco had a short life and ended up upside-down in Victoria harbour when its pilot, Stan Berg, crashed during a charter flight. Fortunately, no one was hurt, but the Waco was a write-off.

The company had to perform like barnstormers at the beginning, sending aircraft over to the Gulf Islands or to nearby Bowen Island—anyplace where there were weekenders who might like to charter a plane for fun or to get home. The company's pilots were instructed to buzz the communities a few times and then to land and wait at the dock. Inevitably, some kids would come down to see the planes, and, with the promise of a ride, they would be sent out to sell seats. On these junkets, the time entered into the aircraft logbooks would be fudged to match the amount of business they actually per-formed. Sylvester had a shortcut for every situation.

79

THIS SYLVESTER WAS NO PUSSYCAT

Left: A series of misadventures assailed Sylvester's BC Airlines in the early years. This factory new Luscombe 8E was run over by a taxiing airliner. GEORGE WILLIAMSON PHOTO

Right: BC Airline's "Learn-to-Fly" sign at Vancouver airport was the extent of the company's advertising during its 1946 underfunded start-up. GEORGE WILLIAMSON PHOTO

One could not have presumed that from such rocky beginnings, B.C. Airlines would grow to be the largest seaplane operation in the world. However, Bill Sylvester's strong personality, his propensity for hard work and highly developed business acumen, as well as his moneyed and influential friends, were responsible for the company's ultimate success. Along the way, the man succeeded in amusing the industry with his way of handling the chain of events that shaped his and the airline's growth.

There were many stories about Sylvester's experiences. They all poked fun at the man's personal idiosyncrasies. Bill's strategy of protecting the aircraft from corrosion with a liberal application of some black gunk to the entire aircraft brought a lot of laughs from pilots and engineers.

"The planes would be dripping with this stuff," recalled George Williamson, Sylvester's chief charter pilot during those early years. "Everybody got fouled with the stuff—pilots and passengers alike. One day, I was launching one of the Luscombe sea-planes with our unique beaching gear. Since it was necessary to 'hand-prop' those early planes, it was customary to do this on dry land. We would then roll the aircraft down the ramp with the engine running, and jump onto the pontoon as the plane was launched. This system involved hanging onto the tail until the last moment," Williamson recalled.

On this day Sylvester had sprayed the stuff all over the tail, and it was dripping and slippery. "I lost my grip, and the plane went motoring down the ramp with me running close behind,"

This racy Globe Swift low wing monoplane was a popular addition to BCAL's fleet of rental aircraft. The "Swift" was involved in a tragic accident when "ditched" off shore near Bellingham WA. A young woman passenger drowned when attempting to swim ashore.

Williamson explained. "I had to leap onto the tail and tried to climb up the slippery fuselage onto the wing. Covered in this black, slippery junk, I then had to step onto the narrow engine cowling behind that whirling prop and make it down onto the float. I made it, but it was sure scary. Sylvester thought it was the funniest thing he had ever seen."

Not all the "funny things" happened to Sylvester's pilots. Despite having a bare 115 hours of flying time, Bill did some of the charter flying himself. On a very famous occasion, he flew one of the Luscombes into a logging camp in Bute Inlet to pick up a logger. Taxiing out into a strong gusting wind and with a passenger aboard, Sylvester was forced to taxi a long way down the inlet in order to have a suitable takeoff run into wind. Unknown to him, one

of the float-compartment covers had fallen off and water slopped into it, causing the aircraft to slowly roll over onto its back.

Sylvester and his passenger made it out the door onto the spreader bar of the upturned floats without getting wet. However, it wasn't long before an icy blast, borne out of the local glaciers, had the two men shivering with incipient hypothermia. They were now well out of sight of the camp and drifting down the inlet. It would soon be getting dark, and both men knew their plight was a serious one—they would not last the night in this bitter cold.

Sylvester's passenger figured he could swim to shore, but Bill knew that the only thing colder than the wind was this water—he convinced the distraught man to hang on. Darkness engulfed them, and after five miserable hours, the two men were near collapse from exposure when they heard the sound of a motorboat coming up the inlet. Waiting until the sound was abeam their position, Sylvester pulled out his Zippo lighter and a handful of $20 bills. The little blaze from the bills was so insignificant that there was only a chance in a million that the flame would be seen. But the boat operator caught sight of something out of the corner of his eye. When he powered

81

back and turned toward the light, he heard the two men's feeble yells. They were saved and the boat operator, a young logger, returned to his camp a hero.

For Bill Sylvester, his much-maligned love of smelly cigars was now justified. The habit had saved his life—otherwise, he wouldn't have carried that Zippo lighter. But nobody at Vancouver airport believed his story; Sylvester would *never* burn a $20 bill.

The story became a classic, and, it formed the cornerstone to many more amusing anecdotes that gave Sylvester the persona of a comic while gaining respect as an astute businessman.

By this time, the little Luscombe seaplanes were proving much too small for the growing business. Bill started to look around for a suitable replacement. Earl McLeod, a pioneer B.C. aviator, was the distributor for a new type of airplane that caught Sylvester's imagination—a flying boat built by Republic Aviation. They called it the "Seabee," and Bill Sylvester made it famous on the coast. He took on the plane as a dealer, and not only put four of them into service but started selling them to other private and commercial operators. Although he loved the versatility of the craft, his pilots learned that the big cabin, the short wings and the low power of its Franklin "pusher" made the Seabee a far from ideal aircraft. Despite early growing pains the little four-place amphibian bearing the popular B.C. Airlines logo was soon to be found at work serving the logging and fish camps and Native villages all along the B.C. coast.

In these formative years for B.C. Airlines, Bill Sylvester's marriage had come unglued, and he moved to Vancouver with his young son, Brian. The gregarious woodcutter, hunter and airline executive met and wooed an attractive younger woman, and the two were married. Sylvester's marital calamities were not over, however. Another classic Sylvester story unfolded.

As he was still working from dawn 'til dark and even into the wee hours of the night, Sylvester was hard-pressed to be attentive to his new wife. Every so often his conscience would get the better of him, and he would turn to a young pilot he had just hired. "Hey Lawrence," he would yell to Lawrence Mantie. "Here's 50 bucks—take my wife to dinner and a show—I gotta work tonight." Lawrence complied with his boss's wishes so often that the inevitable happened—the young pilot and Bill's young wife became an item, and Sylvester was on his own again.

The snickers around the airport resulting from this tragicomedy had hardly subsided when Bill suffered a further loss. This time, it was not a joke. His son, Brian, now a pilot flying for a logging company, was killed in a crash on Vancouver Island's Muchalat Lake. Bill never really recovered from this tragedy, and despite the growing success of the airline, he began to lose interest in his enterprise. John Howroyd, whose father was a well-known Victoria pilot, tells the last and possibly the funniest of stories that brings the man out of the pages of history.

"Bill was always quick to tell you how much he paid for things," said Howroyd. "He would be amazed not only at the high price but that he could now afford to pay for such luxuries—he was incredulous of his own success, but also proud of himself." Howroyd walked into Sylvester's house one day and caught the airline founder emerging from the shower. "He was absolutely

B.C. Airlines developed floatplane bases all over the B.C. coast and employed a variety of aircraft types. The Luscombes and Seabees gave way to Norseman, Beaver and Otter aircraft as the company grew. When the airline split up, the various bases were sold off individually, giving birth to many new coastal air services.

84

stark naked, wearing nothing but his cigar and a pair of new boots, purchased at George Straith's exclusive Victoria men's shop. Totally oblivious of how ridiculous he looked, he regaled me with the story of what an extravagant price he had paid for these boots. All the while, he was clumping around the house in the buff," laughed Howroyd.

In 1959 Bill Sylvester sold B.C. Airlines to a Danish financier, Paul Tak, and local pioneer aviator, Maurice McGregor. The airline was a going concern at this time; it had expanded, with the boom years of the province, from a humble flying school in Vancouver to a network of charter operations located all over the B.C. coast. It operated a fleet of Norseman and Beaver bush planes larger than Sylvester could ever have imagined when he first bought those two little Luscombes 20 years earlier. His decision to sell was based, primarily, on the growing workload of procedures he

would refer to as "government bullshit." The days of heading up the coast in his favourite Seabee to pick up a couple of loggers while puffing on his cigar were long gone. He was bored with the routine, the red tape and the lack of challenge.

"Good riddance," said the now-wealthy founder of the biggest seaplane operation in the world. Then, immediately, he applied for a Class 4 charter licence out of Victoria International Airport under the name of Victoria Flying Services. Nobody was really surprised—Sylvester wasn't known for sitting around. He got the licence on August 29, 1959, and that day phoned his old competitor, Lloyd Michaud, of Vancouver's U-Fly, and placed an order for three new Cessna aircraft: a 150, a 172 and a 180 on floats. Sylvester was back.

John Howroyd, whose father, Joe, was now a shareholder of and the chief pilot for the operation, revealed that Victoria Flying Services was never a financial success. "Bill's old cohorts, Stan Scurrah and Eric Cox, were involved, along with Bill's roommate from those early days, Morris Kersey. They hired Gordie Jeune as chief flying instructor and Bill Cove as a charter pilot. My mother, Iris Howroyd, ran the office and like the rest of them worked day and night to

Sylvester was hard-pressed to stay retired. Following the sale of B.C. Airlines, he very quickly started a new flying operation from his home airport at Victoria. However, Victoria Flying Services was reported to be an "old boys' club" rather than a money-maker. Here, Bill Sylvester turns over the keys for the Cessna in the background to the local car dealer, who, in turn, supplied Bill with his famous T-Bird. Sylvester was ever the deal-maker.

COURTESY JOAN SYLVESTER,
PHOTOGRAPHER BILL
HALKETT

get the company flying. It was an old boy's club," laughed the young Howroyd, who remembered being paid $250 per month for 250 hours of work. The pilots at VFS were earning a big $3 an hour, but they all loved it. And Sylvester was back, fired up with a sense of challenge again. His powder-blue Thunderbird could be seen at the hangar day and night.

Throughout his career, Sylvester was known for his homely proverbs and sayings: "It's not worth anything unless you can own it yourself," was an old saw that had obviously worked for him. Another favourite told its own story: "If you have a problem, fix it." And one was somewhat personal but always brought a laugh: "I've got to quit smoking, drinking and going up stairs."

In 1976, Bill was laid low with a stroke, which left him speechless but mobile. For months he lived in a terrible silence, his eyes displaying the agony of an active man unable to endure this prison. In the light of his own slogans Bill had a problem, and, as always, he solved it. Bill Sylvester stopped smoking cigars, drinking whisky and going up stairs on July 19, 1976.

7

NO TIE NO FLY

Pilots were not always good businessmen, and good businessmen were rarely pilots. Norm Gold was one of the exceptions—he loved to fly but he also loved to turn a good deal and run a tight ship. It is suspected that the deal became more important than the romance of flight as he juggled and wheeled and dealed AirWest Airlines into the major leagues.

Back when he was starting out in the airline business with two hundred bucks to his name and a skeptical banker across the desk, Norm Gold couldn't find a newspaper reporter interested in his plans. Much later, when he had parleyed his company, AirWest Airlines, into the biggest third-level carrier on the B.C. coast, Gold couldn't beat off the press with a club.

"Normy," as he was then called, did battle with the Teamster's Union in his day, and that was bound to get you in the papers. His airline had also grown from a single-plane operation to 21 aircraft. That fleet included 11 turbine-powered Twin Otters and two

turbine-modified Grumman Goose. Along the way he had inhaled two major carriers in the area—Don McGillvery's Nanaimo Airlines and the former B.C. Airlines operation at Port Hardy, on the north end of Vancouver Island.

"Nothing about flying airplanes qualifies a person to run a business," Normy stated during an interview early in his retirement years. "That's where I had an advantage," he added, referring to the fact that he was a businessman long before he got involved with airplanes.

In 1945, when Norm Gold came out of the air force, his military duties as a navigator had left him with that itch for airplanes known to aviators as the "bug." Like all returning servicemen, he was in

88

some doubt about what he wanted to do, and for a short time he returned to his pre-war job as a welder at Burrard Shipyards. This job was cut short, because his grandfather needed help with the family's chain of bakeries. The young man went to Nanaimo to learn that trade and was soon managing the Powell River branch of the family business.

Gold now resumed his interest in airplanes and took flying lessons to gain his commercial pilot's licence. He helped establish a flying club in Powell River, where he instructed students in ground-school courses and became active in promoting a modern airport for the coastal town.

"During those early years, my wife and I were running a restaurant and I was teaching ground school and flying a lot. I didn't plan on being in the airline business," Gold admitted, "but along comes a guy by name of Roy Brett, from Chilliwack, and he has an airline licence but no airplane—well, what is a man going to do?"

Norm Gold bought the licence from Brett and purchased a Piper Clipper and an old Seabee flying boat. At this point in his career, Norm had $200 to his name, but he also had three restaurants. The cash flow from those enterprises paid down the cost of the planes.

"Growth was very slow with those little planes," Gold admitted, explaining that he was doing much of the flying himself while continuing to work the cafés. "It was only when I established a scheduled service between Comox, on Vancouver Island, and Powell River using two twin-engine Apaches that I figured a guy could make a good living in the airline business."

Norm Gold, the businessman, had it figured: "Small airplanes—high frequency," and it was a theory that ultimately paid off for this latter-day pioneer. Proof of its validity showed up in the numbers after a year's operation: his competitor, Pacific Western Airlines, carried 2,000 passengers between Comox and Powell River in big DC-3s, whereas Gold carried 6,500 people in his two little Piper Apaches, flying under the name of Powell River Airways. Gold's key to equipment utilization and profits has since been employed by many other small air carriers, for whom it has worked as well as it did for this entrepreneur when he started up his airline in 1959.

The slogan "No Tie No Fly" was Norm's admonishment to his newly hired pilots. "Damned if I want a bunch of scruffy bush-pilot types flying my passengers," he said. Norm made the policy stick with pilot Al Campbell when he fired that pilot for removing

AirWest's original Twin Otter CF–AWC takes off from Vancouver's waterfront. Norm Gold's airline modernized the downtown to downtown advantage of seaplanes and provided scheduled Twin Otter service from Vancouver to Victoria and Nanaimo cities on Vancouver Island. Later, Baxter Aviation would challenge this service with smaller planes flown more frequently—a concept first introduced by the ever innovative Norm Gold himself.

his tie while employed by the Powell River–based airline. Campbell became Norm's biggest competitor when he stormed out, tieless, and set up shop in nearby Sechelt under the name of Tyee Air (or should that read, Tie-eh Air?). Campbell would become famous in his own right, operating Tyee for the next 35 years, but Normy remained adamant. "Too bad about Al. He would have done a lot better wearing a tie."

Norm Gold was not an easy man to work for, but his keen business sense kept him ahead of the game. By 1965, he had his eye out to acquire other little airlines to amalgamate with Powell River Airways. He had added another credo to his repertoire: "Operate close to your passenger's

destinations." This latest observation was based on the fact that seaplanes could usually get closer to town than could wheeled aircraft operating out of airports. No more significant proof of this was the harbour at the "Hub City" of Nanaimo, on Vancouver Island, with service to downtown Vancouver, on the mainland. On the strength of this conviction he bought out Don McGillvery's Nanaimo Airlines, which was operating a little Cessna 170 and a Beaver on floats out of Nanaimo's downtown harbour. Gold was delighted with this acquisition, for it put him right where he wanted to be— serving two major population centres with what he would now call "downtown service." He envisioned lawyers, doctors, salesmen and other business-men climbing over each other to get on the first flight at daybreak, eager to do a day's business in the big city and yet be home for dinner that evening. He was right again, and he named his new airline just what it was: AirWest.

In the old railway area adjacent to Vancouver harbour, AirWest opened a floatplane terminal and put out the word to residents of both cities that this new harbour-to-harbour service was available. In Nanaimo, the company opened offices in the Malaspina Hotel and established its own exclusive seaplane dock. In the evenings, the company floatplanes were stored at Quesnel Lake, close to Nanaimo, where the company had acquired a mainte-nance hangar and docking facility. During its early days, AirWest operated a single Cessna 180 on this route, but by 1969 the company had four Beavers and a Single Otter dedicated to harbour-to-harbour flights. Passenger volume topped 16,800 by 1970, and Normy's then base manager and pilot-in-charge, Dave Nowzek, stated that each year showed up to a 15 percent increase in people carried. With the success of the downtown flights, 50 percent of the revenue generated was attributed to the growing charter flights out of the Hub City on Vancouver Island—40 to 50 people a day were

now using the AirWest service.

When Norm Gold acquired the licence to operate out of Vancouver, he immediately applied for approval to serve the capital city of Victoria, on the south end of Vancouver Island. He figured that since the smaller city of Nanaimo had proven viable, that big centre of government down in Victoria would be a shoo-in for harbour-to-harbour service. He was right, of course, but the Canadian Transport Commission (CTC), which ruled on such applications, did not have a business concept like Norm's. It turned him down flat. That august group of political appointees, based in Ottawa, were not known for their business acumen and were often thought to be more than a little unsure of exactly where B.C. was located.

But if they thought for a moment that they had got rid of "Normy," they were in for a shock. Many depositions and many trips to Ottawa resulted in the CTC's reluctant decision to extend what it labelled an "experimental licence" to AirWest to operate into Victoria's harbour.

"How do you talk a banker into backing an 'experimental licence?'" cried Norm. "Banks don't get involved in temporary situations." That Norm Gold finally convinced the CTC to issue the proper piece of paper is a

Norm Gold (left) with lawyer, Rich Welters, ferried this turbo-converted Grumman Goose from England to Vancouver. On the first leg to Iceland the aircraft had a flameout and arrived in Iceland on one engine. AWH was operated by AirWest for several years with the turbine engines but was, later, converted back to R985 piston engines. The aircraft was destroyed in a crash in Rivers Inlet in 1987. PHOTO COURTESY BARRY GOLD

great tribute to the man's tenacity, because the then minister of transport, Don Jamieson, was personally against the project. "Jamieson figured that such a service should be held back until de Havilland Canada had their new DHC-6 Twin Otter in the air, and then a major carrier like PWA would be more suitable for serving Victoria," explained Gold. "It seems we trumped their ace," he laughed.

Jamieson was right about the Twin Otter. It was the right aircraft for such a service, and, in fact, Norm Gold would prove to be the right man to initiate the service. "We had spent a lot of time investigating how to operate turbine-powered aircraft in a saltwater environment," said Gold. "We" meant

engineers Dave Evans and Malcolm Campbell, who, with Norm, had worked out an engine freshwater flushing system and reverse position air-intake, which is now standard for turbine-powered aircraft operating off salt water. "We put our ideas in the bank for a while until we had the money to invest in a Twin Otter." During these years Norm attributed the success of AirWest to a group he called "the terrible four": "Irene Nerfa, Ed Green, Dave Evans and Malcolm Campbell ran the airline, and I just opened the doors in the morning and locked them at night."

Gold admitted to one big error in business judgement in 25 years of operation: "I bought that damned fool

The past and present at Victoria Harbour: The CPR steamship Princess Marguerite occupies the background in this photo of AirWest's Victoria base. The Marguerite was once the preferred method of transportation between Vancouver and the capital city. PHOTO COURTESY BARRY GOLD

operation up at Port Hardy." Port Hardy was a former B.C. Airlines base that used amphibious Beavers and Otters and Grumman Goose flying boats operating off the runways of the local airport. These airplanes flew into the many float camps and water-based communities of the area and provided a feeder service for PWA, which operated DC-3 airliners between Port Hardy and Vancouver.

"An operation like that requires very tight management control, or you can go bust—those amphibians carry fewer passengers, burn more gas and have an additional maintenance consideration

with that fancy undercarriage. It just takes one damned pilot to forget to put his wheels down or to pull them up and you've got a wipeout."

Gold, a hands-on businessman, reluctantly put his faith in pilot Jack (Blackie) Apsouris and appointed him manager for that Port Hardy base. Blackie recalled the situation that faced him when he arrived at the North Island airport: "Things were not bad— they were bloody awful," he remembered. "When I got there, the base manager was nowhere to be found—he had a drinking problem and wasn't on the job. Also, there were a

The first de Havilland Dash 7 STOL airliner off the assembly line was delivered to Norm Gold by de Havilland officials. Gold's wonderful plan to operate it from a STOL-port to be constructed off Spanish Banks was shot down by Vancouver's City Council—Norm sold the Dash 7.

DEHAVILLAND CANADA
PHOTO

couple of green pilots trying to fly in the most demanding flying country in B.C. You had to know your way around in that country with the morning fogs and heavy rainfall common to the area." The base had already lost one Beaver—finding only the fuel float transmitter washed up onto a beach—so Blackie quickly located experienced pilots and appointed a new base manager.

"By the time I got things under control, Norm got fed up and sold the operation to Alert Bay Air Service (ABAS), so I cut my tie in half and mailed it to him with my resignation." Blackie couldn't remember exactly which half of the tie he had mailed. "I think the part with the knot in it," he grinned.

The first Twin Otter came on the line in the fall of 1971. The company bought a trade-in, which de Havilland had rebuilt. It was registered appropriately as CF-AWA, and gained the immediate attention of the press as Twin Otter service was initiated between Vancouver, Victoria and Nanaimo harbours. This was the only purchase the airline would ever make directly from de Havilland Canada. Future aircraft would be obtained from other airlines all over the world and rebuilt in the company's now highly developed maintenance facility at the

Vancouver airport. At the high point in AirWest's history, the company was operating 11 of the 14-passenger Twin Otter seaplanes.

During the development of the de Havilland STOL (Short Take-off and Landing) program, Norm Gold's entrepreneurial skills led him to join, with Japanese interests, in a floating STOL–Port concept. The plan envisioned a floating runway installed offshore near the Spanish Banks area of Vancouver harbour. Wheeled aircraft would land here to supply passengers to AirWest's floatplanes. For this short-lived idea, he purchased the first de Havilland Dash 7 STOL airliner. "However, the concept never got off the ground or the water with the City Fathers," quipped Gold. He ultimately sold off the Dash 7.

One of the most significant aspects of AirWest's Twin Otter operations was its solution to engine saltwater corrosion. After observing the problems encountered by Alaska Airlines with its turbine-powered Goose aircraft, AirWest engineers reversed the Goose's air-intake scoop from bottom to topside. For the Twin Otter, the factory-built wash ring system was utilized religiously every night.

"We made a deal with engine builder Pratt & Whitney right from the beginning," explained Gold, "that their operational insurance would apply to our engines on the basis of our established maintenance policy. They went along with it and we flushed those engines, hot, every night of their lives. This was a freshwater flush, because we had determined that the builder's Turco Soap being recommended was actually the cause of some of the corrosion problems. The hot wash we were performing was more expensive, but it was very successful."

Throughout the operation of Gold's AirWest, the Canadian Brotherhood of Railway and Transport Workers (CBRT) had been the main labour union. Apart from contract negotiations every two years, the CBRT had been what Gold described as a reasonable organization to deal with. But many of the employees didn't see it that way. Norm Gold demanded a high level of achievement from employees

and was reputed to push pilots unmercifully, insisting that they fly under questionable weather and flight conditions. The dissident employees sought the services of the Teamsters Union, which had a reputation for being a tough act.

All hell broke loose for the now-beleaguered airline entrepreneur. Demands were made that the airline employ cabin attendants when 12 or more passengers were being carried, and seniority considerations were rained on Norm from all directions. "One day the engineers signed out the fleet as airworthy, and the next day they cited the entire fleet as 'unsafe to fly.' How do you figure that happens?" Gold asked, shaking his head in recollection of those troubled times. "There was even a report that one of the pilots ate his compass deviation card to prove that his plane was unserviceable."

In the ensuing labour battle that engulfed AirWest, Gold stood firm against what he termed a "trucking contract," in which it was demanded that seniority rule in the appointment of new captains. Gold insisted that although seniority was a consideration, the chief pilot would decide who was fit to perform as pilot in command. "Not so," said Local 213, and the strike was on. "I won that battle but lost the war," admitted Gold, sadly. The union did back down on the seniority issue, but the bitterness of the strike, which lasted a full six months, left Gold with little enthusiasm for continuing in the airline business.

The crash of one of his Twin Otters in Vancouver's Coal Harbour put the cap on his gloom. It had been caused by a mechanical problem in the Twin Otter's control system. Although the manufacturer had anticipated the flaw, the level of urgency it employed to advise operators caused the problem. What should have been an urgent "Airworthiness Directive (AD)," requiring the immediate grounding and inspection of the aircraft, was handled, instead, in a routine manner as a Service Bulletin (SB), which requires attention only during the next routine inspection of the aircraft. Though this procedural error was ultimately cited as the cause of several accidents, including AirWest's, the damage was done. The accident had seriously affected AirWest's reputation with the flying public.

Gold was very bitter when, after two years of taking the heat for the death of those 14 passengers, a two-inch column on the back page of a local newspaper announced the findings of the Transportation Safety Board. "I was not totally unhappy that at this moment Jimmy Pattison came along with

an offer to purchase the airline." Norm Gold and Jimmy Pattison started discussing the sale of the airline in 1978, and by the next year had hammered out a deal, which was formally announced in 1980. The Pattison Group took over AirWest as the first acquisition of seven coastal air services to be amalgamated under the name of AirBC. Norm retired to his home on Salt Spring Island.

As those red-and-white Twin Otters flew over his Gulf Island retreat, the man who could still remember the words to the hit song "Downtown" often wondered aloud if they were making any money at it. Still the old "Normy."

AirBC ultimately sold off its harbour-to-harbour service to a new company with the famous old name of West Coast Air. This airline now competes with Harbour Air in providing Twin Otter service between Vancouver and Victoria. In addition, Baxter Aviation, employing Norm Gold's theory of "small airplanes—frequent service," flies seven Beaver flights per day between Nanaimo and Vancouver, competing with Harbour Air's Twin Otter service. The American carrier Kenmore Air flies a scheduled operation into Victoria harbour from a downtown seaplane base on Lake Union in Seattle, Washington.

We think Normy was on to something.

8

THE CHICKEN HAWK AIRLINE

Brothers have figured large in the flying business—who can forget Orville and Wilbur? Although Mr. and Mrs. Michaud's two boys didn't put their caps on backward when they flew, they did make B.C. aviation history. Lloyd Michaud bought into Gilbert's Flying School in 1938, on the eve of the Second World War, and rejuvenated it at the war's end. His brother joined him, and together they left an impressive legacy as aviation entrepreneurs.

A white doily protects both pilot seats, the floor is spotless and there is an absence of dust or grime anywhere in the cabin of this little two-place airplane. Though spotless, the plane is not new—the wear on the rudder pedals suggests that many pilots have flown her, and the tachometer registers 1,500 hours of flight time. The top of the instrument panel is painted in a flat paint, a dark-green colour that extends out to the nose cowlings housing a little 85-horsepower engine. The same paint then carries on down both sides of the aircraft in a tapering speed line delineating the 30-inch-high registration letters CF-DST. The rest of the plane is unpainted aluminum and gleams brilliantly in the sun. That flat paint on the nose of this Cessna model 140 acted as a glare shield to protect the eyes of the many student pilots who learned to fly in this trainer between the years 1945 and 1956.

DST and other shiny new Cessna aircraft were owned by a company named Vancouver's U-Fly, whose flying school was based on the south side of Vancouver International Airport. The founder of the company, Lloyd Michaud, was also the chief flying instructor. He taught a generation of students how to fly airplanes. It was a joke of the day that if you knocked on

Previous page: PAINTING
(detail) BY GLEN MATTHEWS

Right: Vancouver's U-Fly emerged from the old Gilbert Flying School, which was purchased by Lloyd Michaud just before the Second World War. With the outbreak of war, private flying was curtailed in Canada, and the fleet was placed in storage in Kamloops, B.C. Pictured here in 1947, the popular school had added several then-modern airplanes and was a going concern. The most famous, CF-BAT (facing page), was the early flagship of the fleet.

U-FLY PHOTO

the flight-deck door of any airliner in Canadian skies you would find a captain whom Lloyd had taught to fly. He was revered as the pilot's pilot.

Lloyd had a brother, Aylmer, whom everyone, understandably, called Al. Al was the business guy behind Vancouver's U-Fly, and while he too was a pilot with lots of experience, he much preferred to plot the next move of the fast-growing company than to teach stick and rudder to aspiring airline pilots.

Al met with the Cessna Aircraft Co. very soon after the Second World War and obtained the dealership for Cessna products for western Canada. Cessna became the biggest name in the air, and U-Fly prospered on two fronts,

flight training and new aircraft and parts sales.

In 1956, the Vancouver airport had become a major, and now internationally recognized, airport. Flight training from such a busy field was becoming a problem of convenience and safety. The flying schools were given an ultimatum: quit or get out. The other flying clubs and schools chose to move to the nearby Pitt Meadows airport, but Al and Lloyd had other plans for U-Fly. They sold the flying school to Art Seller at nearby Langley airport, and their aircraft-parts business was sold to a new outfit called Lindair Services. They then set up a well-founded floatplane operation called West Coast Air Services. Al had a

company logo designed and painted on the tail of their new aircraft fleet. That logo incorporated an eagle's head with the "W" of West Coast Air.

Other local airlines and aviators who were disdainful of this new airline invading their turf called the resulting graphic a "chicken hawk," and West Coast Air was immediately dubbed "The Chicken Hawk Airline." It wasn't meant to be a compliment. But those detractors would soon eat their words as the "Chicken Hawk Airline," piloted by the two most experienced aviator/businessmen on the coast, became the definitive floatplane operator in British Columbia. Significantly, they also became the employers of choice for the best and most professional of pilots in the area.

Key to the success of U-Fly and West Coast Air was Al Michaud's contribution to the family endeavours—the early alignment with the Cessna Aircraft Co. Cessna designed and marketed the aircraft that brought general aviation back into peacetime commerce. The sale of new aircraft and a burgeoning parts-supply business became the backbone of the brothers' enterprises.

MARCH, 1949

Earnings climb, too...

IN YOUR NEW 1949 Cessna 170

YOU CAN'T AFFORD NOT TO HAVE IT!....You'll soon discover that! For this new 4-place All-metal "Family Car of the Air" is invaluable in business....adds to family income as well as family fun!

NEW! Tapered, all-metal wing for improved stability, greater flying control, lower maintenance! NEW, more effective wing flaps for safer landings!

NEW interior styling! Fine upholstery, beautifully tailored! Harmonizing color schemes. Deep, luxurious, roomy, comfortable seats.

140 M.P.H. TOP SPEED 145 H.P. Continental Engine. Over 300-mile range. Wide doors. Wide seat! Wheel pants extra.

A BIGGER PAY CHECK plus more time to go places - do things - have fun! This remarkable new plane can bring you all that....and more! Business trips will take a fraction of the time they used to. You'll earn more because you'll be WORKING MORE...can cover more ground, get more done. And you'll week and visit vacation at places which used to be out of range. For this plane is safe, easy to fly! Its 4-place luxury and comfort, 120 m.p.h. cruising speed, make every trip a pleasure...and operating costs per passenger are a fraction of ordinary travel costs!

USE THIS COUPON or See Your Nearest Cessna Dealer

Cessna Airport Co., Dept. CA-3, Wichita, Kansas.

Cessna 120-140 Roomy, 2-place, economical planes at a

Cessna 190-195 Luxurious, 4-5 place personal or company

A Cessna Ad of 1949 indicates the family car concept

"The Cessna 180 mounted on floats had a lot to do with our going into the airline and charter business," said Al Michaud. "Until the 180 came along, the Norseman, and later the Beaver, were the definitive charter floatplanes. There wasn't an airplane of a size to handle the two- and three-passenger charters. The 180 filled this need economically and provided a fast and comfortable modern airplane that handled well on floats."

The Cessna 180 and West Coast Air arrived on the scene at the same time,

and the airline commenced business with three of the new-model Cessnas mounted on locally built CAP 3000 floats. Two Beaver floatplanes rounded out the fleet. A former student of Vancouver's U-Fly, Jack Stelfox, was appointed chief pilot, and Stu Phillips, a legendary pilot from early Queen Charlotte Airlines days, became operations manager of the new company.

The Michaud brothers had by this time moved their operations from their original field office to a more appropriate establishment on Vancouver's Airport Road South. From this location, they managed both their airline and the sale of new Cessna aircraft. The Michauds also built a dispatch centre and passenger terminal beside the seaplane ramp adjacent to the river and a maintenance base with engineer Gordon Peters handling all the fleet mechanical work plus providing outside aircraft maintenance services. To round out the company's needs and those of the local aviation community, a radio shop was also established at this time. The Chicken Hawk Airline was now set up in the diversified manner that Al Michaud knew would carry it through the usual thick-and-thin business conditions typical of the charter flying business.

Although West Coast Air Services took on a much more sophisticated image than had its predecessor,

When the Cessna 180 on floats came on the scene it played an important role for coastal airlines—the perfect airplane for those many two or three passenger charters. Dubbed, the "Spam Can" by irreverent pilots, due to its mass production, it was a pleasant airplane to fly. As the first coastal operator to use the speedy little plane, West Coast Air Services claimed that it was responsible for their immediate success.

Vancouver's U-Fly, one characteristic of the Michaud brothers' operations never changed—the company was a good employer. In an industry with more than its share of borderline operators, the Michauds were gentlemen and lived up to a reputation of consideration for both their customers and their staff. Pilots flew new airplanes that were well maintained. Dispatch, office, maintenance and dock personnel were treated as important members of a happy family all working to the same end.

Doreen Kozak, the company's first dispatcher (later employed in the same chair with Harbour Air) tells a story that illustrates the good fellowship: "I started to work for West Coast in 1956. I was hired as a dispatcher. Of course, as the new kid in the company I drew the early morning shift, which started work at 7 A.M. On my first

A generation of airline pilots was trained by Lloyd Michaud, who gave up a senior pilot's position with CP Air to launch his new flying school. U-Fly was ultimately sold, and Lloyd, with brother Al, went on to found another legacy, West Coast Air Services.

DOREEN KOZAK COLLECTION

102

morning I found the doors unlocked and the lights on, and the janitor was sweeping the floors and cleaning up the office. I made the coffee and offered the janitor a cup as well. He happily accepted and laid aside his broom to join me. This became something of a ritual for the seven days of my shift, and this gentleman and I became quite good friends. I then went on afternoon shift and was surprised to find my coveralls friend in and around the offices during that shift as well.

One day, I saw him sitting in Al Michaud's office, and my curiosity got the better of me. I asked the office accountant what the janitor was doing in the boss's office. The accountant burst out laughing and introduced me to Lloyd Michaud, the erstwhile janitor. He thought it was a great joke. We remained good friends, and I worked for West Coast right to the end of its days."

Russ Baker's Pacific Western Airlines (PWA) had grown into a large airline by this time, but despite its stature as a major carrier it continued to operate seaplanes on the coast and in the interior of British Columbia. In 1966 PWA offered to sell its floatplane operations in Vancouver, Nelson, Prince George and Kamloops to West Coast Air. Al Michaud met with executives Dick Laidman and Don Watson to negotiate the deal.

Al Michaud told the story this way: "We had quite a long and detailed discussion on the value of these bases and had arrived at a dollar figure with which I was comfortable and which they considered to be rock bottom. I asked for a recess in order to have a directors' meeting over at West Coast's offices. I left the two PWA people for what I told them would be about one hour. I walked over to brother Lloyd's office and explained the deal to him.

WALLY RUSSELL · AL. EDEN · RICHARD GRAY · JACK MALESHEWSKI · IAN BLACK · N
· NORM ROGERS · NOBBY HEIDER · WALT WINBERG · CHUCK FORD · JOHN
BC AIR LINES TOM GLAISTER · RUSS M°KINNON **Pacific Western** GO
HN BOAKE · GORD M°KENZIE · ROY JONES · HARRY BROWN · J
KI · JIM DUNCAN · TERRY WILLY · GORDIE RUSSELL · LEN BRYAN · HOWIE J
OM TOMLIN · RICK NELSON · STAN KAARDAL · TOM LEE · BOB POGUE · BA
JRR · ROY REAVILLE · M ANSON · JIM WILSON ·
CROISDALE · KURT M STU. SPURR · MI
RAFF MONT FRED HARMS
DIXON W
AirBC TC JIM PEARSE
KURT MILLER
E JAMIESON BILL COVE
E SHAFFER · H TERRY
BILL JANSEN · G FRE
LL WICKE ROY R

AGAINST A BACKGROUND THAT COULD BE BELLA COOLA,
BELLA-BELLA OR OCEAN FALLS, A GRUMMAN MALLARD
RE-FUELS FOR HER LAST TRIP HOME. IN TWENTY YEARS
OF SERVICE TO BC COASTAL COMMUNITIES, THESE FLYING
BOATS SERVED UNDER FOUR FLAGS AND EARNED THE
AFFECTION OF MANY PILOTS, SOME OF WHOM ARE NAMED
HERE.   - JACK SCHOFIELD 1982.

H HARRISON · STAN LEIGH · WAYNE KAART · JIM PEARSE · BILL WICKETT · HARR
NTY FETTERLY · BARBARA WARSHAWSKI · DOUG STEWART · GREG GRAFF · DOUG B
JUSTIN de GOUTIERE · JIM WILSON · BOB P STAN LEIGH · WALL
KE SHARETT · DAVE STRONACH · HUGH FRASER · RED **West Coast Air** SDALE · GORDIE RUSS
· DOUG. STUART · BILL WADDINGTON ·

Against a background that could be Bella Coola, Bella-Bella or Ocean Falls, a Grumman Mallard
re-fuels for her last trip home. In twenty seven years of service to BC coastal communities, the flying
boats served under four flags and earned the affection of many pilots, some of whom are named here.

The Chicken Hawk Airline was soon setting new standards for third-level air carriers. The company operated Twin Otters on scheduled service between Vancouver and Victoria and employed six Grumman Mallard flying boats on coastal routes between Prince Rupert and Vancouver. West Coast Air was one of Jimmy Pattison's later acquisitions in the formation of AirBC. At the time it was thought that Pattison could have limited his acquisitions to West Coast alone, because its route structure was all he needed to provide a comprehensive regional service.

DOREEN KOZAK
COLLECTION

104

He approved of it, so I walked back and told the two PWA guys that it was a deal. That director's meeting took less than 30 minutes, and don't think those two PWA executives weren't amazed."

The Canadian Transport Commission (CTC) ruled on such transfers of services, and it was protocol for them to allow other airlines to contest the transfer. Norm Gold's AirWest Airlines was quick to mount a bevy of lawyers at the hearing intent on discrediting Michaud's ability to perform.

"There are many many dollars involved in this transaction," stated Brian Williams, the principal AirWest lawyer at the subsequent court hearing. "How does a little outfit like yours intend to pay?"

"I thought I would just write out a cheque," replied Michaud. This brought a snicker from the court and caused that lawyer to sit down. West Coast won the day.

With the new bases acquired from PWA, the airline gained three additional Beaver floatplanes and was now playing in the big leagues—just where Al Michaud wanted to be. His principal competitor at this point was B.C.

The charter operation that other airlines were quick to disdain became the largest and most professional of them all. The short-lived Fairchild Husky in West Coast colours here discharges prospectors onto a glacial lake.
DOREEN KOZAK COLLECTION

Airlines, who aspired to become British Columbia's regional air carrier.

"B.C. Airlines became dedicated to their scheduled services and wanted out of the charter business," explained Al. "They started to pass all their charter work over to us, and we were very happy to get it," he laughed. "With our own passengers and the work passed over to us by B.C. Airlines, we became the largest third-level carrier on the coast while B.C. Airlines flew into oblivion."

In the days before deregulation, airlines were not permitted to parallel the service of a competitor. To expand its route structure or class of service, West Coast Air would find it necessary to take over a competitor's airline through a buyout. These transactions were the subject of onerous regulations and were undertaken only by those with the patience to wait and the staff to handle the mountain of required paperwork. West Coast had these requirements and commenced a series of takeovers that would make them the largest of all such air carriers in British Columbia. In 1970, West Coast acquired Nanaimo-based Pacific

Coastal Airlines, which gave the company a significant U.S. Navy contract and a charter facility at Nanaimo. This was followed by the purchase of Staron Flight of Vancouver, then Trans Provincial Airlines' base at Ocean Falls and, most significantly, a licence held by Victoria Flying Services permitting West Coast to now compete with AirWest flying into Victoria harbour.

West Coast's chicken hawk logo was now being sported on the tails of many Twin Otter seaplanes and Grumman Mallard flying boats, which with each buyout were joined by Beavers, Single Otters and Cessna floatplanes. The Mallard fleet, first established by Pacific Western Airlines to service the entire coast from Prince Rupert south to Vancouver, was expanded, under the Michaud brothers stewardship, from three to six aircraft. These magnificent flying boats were ultimately retired after 27 years of yeoman service to B.C.'s coastal communities.

The takeover business works both ways. Another group had West Coast Air Services in their sights—a corporate entity known as Cromarty Holdings. In 1978, this consortium of investors made an offer to the Michauds that the brothers couldn't refuse. West Coast Air was sold, but the new owners wisely kept Al Michaud on in a management capacity and as a minor shareholder. It was an interesting time for non-aviation people to become involved in this airline because AirWest, piloted by West Coast Air's bitter adversary, Norm Gold, was making things hot for the Chicken Hawk Airline.

When West Coast Air acquired the licence permitting scheduled service into Victoria harbour, there was a proviso attached that its aircraft must always land first at a Gulf Islands destination inbound, and then again outbound, from Victoria. AirWest, which did not like sharing this lucrative business, watched West Coast like a hawk. If the West Coast Twin Otter didn't make those mandatory stops, Norm Gold would fire off a complaint to the CTC and demand legal action.

The local press kept Lower Mainland readers well informed about this feud, and it became a subject of amused conversation on the streets of Vancouver and Victoria. When Al Michaud applied to the CTC to have the Gulf Islands destination classed as a "whistle stop," requiring that West Coast Air land only when there was a passenger, he received an intervention from an unexpected source. The complaint was from Jimmy Pattison, B.C.'s most famous entrepreneur, who

The Michaud
brothers, Al and
Lloyd, were
reputed to be the
best of employers.
The two popular
pilots made
employees feel a
part of the family.
Many of those who
flew for West Coast
Air went on to
become leading
figures in the
Canadian aviation
community. Here
Al and Lloyd
embrace one of
their "family."
DOREEN KOZAK
COLLECTION

was then in the process of acquiring
AirWest Airlines.

It is now a matter of record that
Jimmy Pattison went on to acquire a
total of seven B.C. coastal airlines,
including West Coast Air. In 1980,
Pattison's management group amalgamated these seven companies under the
name of AirBC and, in doing so,
created the first homegrown regional
air service in British Columbia. When
the Pattison Group later sold AirBC,
first to Canadian Pacific Airlines and
then withdrew from that deal to nearly
double its money with a sale to Air
Canada, B.C.'s financial hero received a
silent ovation from the entire aviation
industry for having achieved the
takeover coup of the century.

Significant to the legacy of the
Michaud brothers is the fact that the
Chicken Hawk fraternity of former
West Coast Air employees included
many who went on to become the
most successful people in the industry.
These former employees still meet
occasionally to celebrate their years
with the two brothers, Lloyd and Al
Michaud, who have made a significant
contribution to the B.C. coastal
aviation community.

MY RELIEF PILOT RE-DEFINED
THE MEANING OF "THE ROMANCE OF
FLIGHT" — JACK SCHOFIELD
— 2004

SEX AND THE SINGLE ENGINE

There isn't such a thing as a humdrum day with airplanes. Apart from the obvious thrill imparted by flight itself and the power of the machine you have in your control, there is the entertainment provided by the people you fly with—who they are, what they do, where they are going. And, wherever there are people, there is always the possibility of . . . well, let's call them "misunderstandings."

She wore powder-blue satin "short-shorts" and a matching zippered jacket. She was good to look at—the kind of figure a logger, fresh out of 14 days in camp, could dwell upon. She knew all about this and could handle herself. Perched atop the Cessna 185's wing, my recently hired pilot knew that her passengers were taking the measure of her from below, so to speak.

"Can you handle this?" she asked, passing the fuel hose down to the most obvious of the waiting loggers.

"I'm quite sure I can handle it," he said, taking the hose but not his eyes from her. There was a micro-second of electricity between the two before she took charge of the situation.

"Okay, you guys—back in the plane. Next stop Port McNeill."

The three men boarded the aircraft as their attractive pilot cast the line around the forward float strut and pushed off from the dock.

I watched from a short distance down the seaplane dock as she slid into the pilot's seat and cranked over the engine. Hot from the first leg of the trip, the fuel-injected engine was reluctant to start. My new hire wasn't too experienced at starting a hot-injected-type engine, and I could hear that she wasn't advancing the throttle far enough. She was forgetting the instructions from her check ride. But after a few more seconds the engine fired and she was roaring across the water, leaving a fine spray from the Cessna's rooster tail as the plane broke water and climbed in a steep banking turn into Wells Channel. It then levelled off and disappeared behind the hills. I could still hear that supersonic propeller tip, now muffled by the forest, as I climbed into my own aircraft, musing over the events of the past few days.

The pilot had presented herself to me one day about a month after arriving in the area. She wanted me to hire her—she wanted a flying job. She claimed to have 1,200 hours total flying time, with 400 of it on floats.

"My log book is at home in Manitoba," she explained, "but I'll send for it. In the meantime, I could be getting business for you with this other plane." She presented her commercial pilot's licence as proof, so I had no cause to doubt her numbers.

So far, I'd been doing all the flying for the little airline with one seaplane, based out of nearby Shawl Bay. My other Cessna stayed tied up, in storage, here on the dock at Sullivan Bay. It had been a very busy summer, and my one-man airline needed another man—even if it was a woman. I hired her.

It was planned that she would stay at Sullivan Bay with the plane. Our dispatcher, located in Shawl Bay, seven miles downstream, would phone her if we needed the services of the second aircraft. If someone wanted to charter the plane from her at Sullivan Bay, she was to call us to make the arrangments.

"Sounds okay," said the dispatcher, Alan Brown, when I told him the plan. His words were reassuring, but his face told another story. I figured Al was just another tough old retired logger who couldn't visualize a "mere woman" flying seaplanes around this country. Of course, I saw myself as out there on the cutting edge, advancing the cause of women even in the bush, on the mid-coast of British Columbia. This was a man's country, and if you had any doubt about that you just had to ask one of them.

Three Native villages, five logging camps and four sports fishing camps, in addition to several private float camps, depended on my "one-man airline" for transportation, freight and groceries. And this country also had its share of tough guys and drunks who might give a woman a bad time.

"She's pretty gutsy, Al," I assured him, "and I instructed her not to go into Kingcome—that river is too much for an inexperienced pilot after this heavy rainfall."

"Amen," replied Al, still looking doubtful.

Things had been pretty hectic for the past few months. A competitor had opened up 20 miles south at Minstrel Island and was making himself available for my customers whenever I got too busy—he had only to listen out on our radio-phone frequency to learn where to go. With our second airplane on the line, things should become less complicated. Much later I would realize that, before I had hired my new pilot, things had not been complicated at all—she was to redefine the meaning of "complicated" and completely reshape my world.

"If you think you're going to vamp my husband with those shiny pants and that slippery zipper, you've got another think coming, Missy." These words were spat out with vehemence by a logger's wife at one of the local logging camps. She was directing her vitriol toward my new pilot as she followed her down the dock toward the plane.

What's this all about? I thought. And why was the other plane in here in the first place? I had been called in to pick up a passenger from the logging camp at Scott Cove and couldn't understand why my other plane and pilot were here. The look of astonishment must have been plain on my face as I approached the irate wife.

"You'd be better off without that one, Jack," she levelled at me. "Or at least, get her to wear some clothes."

Later, as I taxied out of the bay with my passenger, I ruminated about this turn of events. The angry wife was a good friend and not given to this sort of outburst without reason. My new pilot, flying our second registered plane, BMO, had arrived on the dock a few moments after me, tied up her aircraft and walked the dock toward us. Then all hell broke loose and she had retreated and taken off before I could question her.

"I never called her," said Alan, astonished when I described the events to him later that night. "We've had no need for the second plane so far, and it sure as hell shouldn't have been in Scott Cove." Alan was getting excited. "Why is she out flying around?" he asked.

Good question, I thought, and decided to fly up to Sullivan in the morning to find out what was going on.

The next morning BMO landed in Shawl Bay at the crack of dawn. The lady in question jumped out, all smiles. "Here's your booty," she exclaimed, proffering a sheaf of charter slips and a pile of cash. Bewildered, I took the papers, which proved to represent about $1,600 worth of charter flights, with cash and cheques to support the slips.

"People are just chartering me direct from Sullivan Bay," she continued. "They see the airplane on the dock and want to go. I haven't been able to reach you on the phone, but I just couldn't turn down the business—people are phoning Sullivan Bay for a plane!"

From the look of the tickets she gave me, "people" was mainly the logging camp in Drury Inlet close to Sullivan—a camp from which we had never had business because that company owned its own seaplane. Now, she was flying numerous charters in and out of there and also from camps in nearby Acteon Sound and Seymour Inlet. Her statement that she couldn't reach us on the radio was somewhat valid; radio-telephone reception from Sullivan was notoriously bad. Of course, she had the company VHF frequency, which always worked from the air, so that thinned out her excuses somewhat.

Mollified by the increased business resulting from the positioning of the second plane, I asked her about the fracas at Scott Cove the day before and asked why she was there in the first place. Without missing a beat, she replied: "Look, I was just canvassing for business—I never met that lady before, least of all her husband. But she was loaded for bear, so I just got out of there."

"Maybe you should wear something just a little less provocative," I suggested. This brought forth something of a coy smile. I think she was about to launch into an indignant reference to

sexism and male chauvinism but changed her mind and agreed to dress less revealingly for the logging trade. She never did adopt the company dress code, but on this occasion she did roll down her sleeves. I repeated my earlier admonition not to go into Kingcome under any circumstances, to which she agreed. Then, promising to keep in regular contact, she took off for Sullivan Bay.

I was brought up by a mother and a sister who convinced me that women were a cut above men in the honour department. Mine was the era during which young boys were instructed to always hold doors and stand up for ladies in a crowded bus or on a streetcar. But my mid-Victorian ethics were about to be put to the extreme test.

"I have a little problem." It was "herself" calling me on the radio-phone a week later. "You'd better come up to Sullivan right away."

I jumped into my aircraft and bombed up Sutlej Channel post-haste. Landing on a descending turn around the point, I spotted BMO at the dock, complete with wings, fuselage and tail, so that ended the biggest worry. On closer examination, I found a hole about the size of a grapefruit in the leading edge of the left wing. There was also some distortion to the upper skins on the wing.

"It happened at Kingcome," she admitted. "I just couldn't get hold of you, so I flew in there anyway."

It seems she had landed on the swift-running Kingcome River and got to the dock all right, but with three passengers aboard she had been unable to hot-start the Cessna immediately after turning out into the swift waters. The engine had finally fired when the plane's nose was pointed directly at the opposite shore and she drove the plane at full power onto the beach, punching a hole in the wing on a big stump. She had ordered her passengers out of the plane, which they started to do when the craft suddenly freed itself from the beach and was swept back into the raging waters.

"Everybody back in," she ordered. As the passengers complied, she put the boots to it and took off downriver and into the air.

She proceeded to fly her anxious passengers to their destination at Alert Bay. Then, despite the fact that the hole in the wing had opened up considerably from the effects of the flight, she brought two more passengers aboard and flew them back to their camp. The damaged plane was then flown to its base at Sullivan.

I fired her. She said she understood.

An aircraft engineer working with a local heli-logging outfit inspected the wing and assured me it was structurally okay. He stuffed the hole with an old onion sack from the cookhouse and reformed the leading edge with—you guessed it—duct tape.

"Fly that down to Vancouver and get it fixed," he said, "It'll be fine."

"Herself" then approached me with the news that she was planning to return to her home in Manitoba. Why not let her fly the plane to Vancouver, where she would leave it with the repair outfit? "That would save you from shutting down the airline while you went to Vancouver, Jack," she said in a conciliatory tone. "It's the least I can do to help out under the circumstances."

As I was booked solid with charters for the next couple of days, it wasn't a bad suggestion. I agreed, adding the proviso that she must stop in at Shawl Bay, first thing in the morning, before proceeding to Vancouver.

The next morning she bid us all adieu. "Goodbye everybody," she said, standing there on the dock at Shawl Bay. "I hope it all works out for you." She waved to all of us assembled on the dock, then taxied out for takeoff.

"She's wearing jeans today, I see," said Alan. "That hard westerly has too much of a bite to it, I guess," he grinned. This remark brought a snicker from Alan's wife and daughter, who had come out to watch BMO take off and overfly the bay with a goodbye waggle of its wings. The plane then took up a heading for Vancouver, riding what was now becoming a strong westerly tailwind.

There was a hard day's flying ahead of me, so I got into it and soon forgot about our "Siren of Sullivan Bay," as we had dubbed our erstwhile pilot. With that tailwind she would be in town and out of our lives in two and a half hours.

An intermittent clunking noise developed up forward in my aircraft during that day. When I returned to Shawl Bay late that afternoon, I pulled all the cowlings and eyeballed the engine for obvious problems, discovering a hairline crack on one of the upright members of the engine mount. I called the company engineer and arranged for him to fly in early the next morning with a new engine mount.

The airline owner flew the engineer and the new mount in to camp at daybreak, and the two of them set to rigging an ingenious method for lifting the engine out of my plane. We all pitched in to help, and by two o'clock had the engine out and hanging, precariously, on a plank over the water. The phone rang.

"Your airplane is sinking over in Hardy Bay," the caller informed me.

"I don't have an airplane in Hardy Bay," I replied. "The only other plane I have is BMO, and it's down in Vancouver, under repair."

"This airplane is BMO," stated the caller. "It has rolled over at the dock here in Port Hardy."

I was stunned. We held a quick conference and decided we could not leave this engine hanging over the water while we flew to BMO's aid in the owner's plane. We would have to button the engine on to the new mount before going anywhere. We fell back to work with a vengeance, each wondering in the privacy of his own mind what in the hell had happened, and developing a slow angry burn as we worked.

The engine safely installed, we took off in the owners' plane for Hardy Bay. My private thoughts were filled with four-letter words that were directed toward a certain female pilot who had just blown away my future.

Hardy Bay marina looked like a lily pond. Hundreds of multicoloured squares floated among the docks and fishing boats. On closer inspection, these turned out to be record jackets, floating up from the open door of BMO, which was now viewed from the dock as she hung upside down, suspended by her floats, with their black bottoms for all to see. I picked up a Bob Dylan jacket and spun it across the bay, cursing aloud. Our engineer, British to

Caught flat-footed with the engine removed, we could not rush to the aid of our other aircraft, reported sinking at the dock in Port Hardy.

the core, went about salvaging the airplane in a totally professional manner.

We found her, with a boyfriend, booked into a local hotel. She had been there for 16 hours, and checking the airplane at the dock was the furthest thing from her mind. When she was made aware of what had happened, her only concern was for all her worldly goods, which she had stored in the plane for the trip to town. They included the record collection now floating in Hardy Bay. She had the gall to suggest that somebody was going to pay for this.

"Somebody has paid," I said.

What I didn't know at the time was the sequence of events that had led to the calamity. The story was told to me later by the chief pilot at the heli-logging show, in Drury Inlet—the camp

BMO had been
recently refurbished
at considerable cost—
not a consideration
of the pilot who
abandoned airman-
ship in favour of an
amorous tryst in a
local hotel. LP record
jackets floated on the
bay like lily pads.

ROLAND SHANKS PHOTO,
NORTH ISLAND GAZETTE

116

where we had been getting all that new business.

"Your lady pilot had something big going on with the camp superintendent," he told me. "He was getting the business, so you were getting the business," he laughed. She had doubled back after leaving Shawl Bay that morning and flown into the Drury Inlet camp to pick up her lover. They had planned to go to town together.

"I watched the whole thing—we all watched the whole thing," explained the helicopter pilot. "She arrived during that hard westerly wind. Nobody else would have attempted to land in that water. We had shut down the helicopters from the logging operation because of the high winds, and all our pilots were lined up on the bank watching her. She hit the water like a ton of bricks."

He reminded me how large the waves get in Drury Inlet in a westerly wind. The narrow inlet simply smokes with swells and white water in a strong west wind. He described how my pilot had hammered the plane into these swells with eight heavy impacts before coming to a stop, then had to take off again because she had passed the dock and couldn't sail back in that heavy water.

"That poor airplane," he said. "No wonder the floats leaked at the dock." The chief pilot then recounted how my ex-employee had finally slammed the plane onto the water and got it to the dock—one pontoon was lifted by the waves onto the planks—then tied it up and left it in that position while she went in search of her superintendent lover.

"In the meantime, the super's wife had got wind of her husband's affair with your pilot. She had informed head office, who had lowered the boom on him. He was in deep trouble and was going nowhere with Miss Fancy Pants."

My informant went on to describe how the now-irate lady pilot went ballistic. She stormed down the ramp to her aircraft, jumped in and blasted off the dock, dragging that left float across the planked deck, then taking off across those bone-shattering swells. She flew a short distance down the inlet and landed again, this time in protected water, beside a large seagoing tug whose skipper had long been publicly expressing his hunger for her physical attentions.

"How about a night in Port Hardy?" brought him over the rail like a French matelot at the *Folies Bergère*.

The farce ended there; the rest is history. In consideration of this chain of events and of the havoc wreaked by my poor judgement, I came to many conclusions—one of which was never to give up my seat on a bus.

9

PAPER BAG PILOT

Dan McIvor is a critic of airplanes that drop pretty red stuff on the unburned parts of a forest fire while the blaze destroys millions of trees. He says it doesn't have to be that way. "Why not stop the fire before it gets away on you?" he asks. Another thing McIvor finds untenable is that the executive branch of the B.C. Forest Service manages the fighting of forest fires. He believes aviation firefighters have a better handle on how to put the blaze out: "Their first thought would be how to put out the fire, not how much it was going to cost." Who is this McIvor guy? Well, those magnificent Martin Mars water bombers hanging off their anchor-buoys on Vancouver Island's Sproat Lake are Dan McIvor's brainchild.

Until 1959, the British Columbia forest industry fought forest fires with stirrup pumps, picks and shovels, bulldozers and manpower—lots of manpower. There was no concept of putting the fire out—it was simply a battle for containment. Thousands of hectares of standing forest were ravaged each year in fires caused by either careless humans or lightning strikes. Educating the public brought a degree of control, but electrical storms were still the major cause of fires. There were many international forest companies at work in B.C. during these years, and two significant homegrown forestry giants, the Powell River Co. and MacMillan Bloedel, promoted the formation of an industry consortium to pool resources and fight this common foe.

British Columbia was not alone in its concern—Ontario's Lands and Forests department was also conducting experiments with water-drops from a specially equipped Beaver aircraft. After seeing the promising results from

Dan McIvor's original idea for aerial firefighting was to drop paper bags full of water on the blaze. Employing a Grumman Goose aircraft, it was modestly successful. "If small airplanes can do it, why not a great big airplane?" The implementation of his idea gained McIvor the Order of Canada and a seat in Canada's Aviation Hall of Fame.

DAN McIVOR PRESS PHOTO

these experiments, the B.C. Forest Service advised the coastal airline operators that it would smile on the airline that equipped an aircraft with custom tanks and made it available for fire control. West Coast Air Services responded immediately and supplied a Beaver fitted out with the required system. The success of this little airplane in controlling small fires was proven on the first application.

Dan McIvor and a small group of enthusiasts figured that if a little plane could put out a small fire, maybe a big plane could put out a big fire. The decision to investigate the use of large aircraft did not come from the top down—it came from the bottom up, and Dan McIvor was the bottom rung on the ladder. So convinced was he of the idea that he took the initiative and started to look for a suitable plane. A close look was given to the Saunders Roe SR-45 "Princess" and the Bristol "Brabazon," both huge aircraft of the day. However, neither type had been

Before the Mars became available, many other giant aircraft were considered. The Saunders Roe "Princess" was one of those, but it was "one of a kind" and thus not a suitable choice.

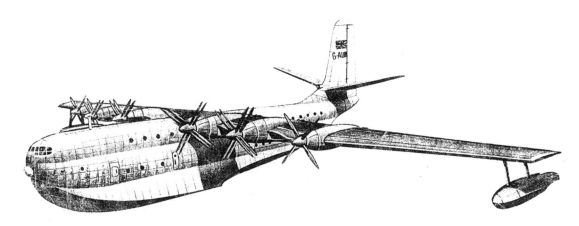

produced in sufficient quantities, so the search went on. One day, a friend casually mentioned that the U.S. Navy had just retired those famous Martin Mars flying boats and planned to auction them off.

"Maybe I didn't do a double take," laughed McIvor. "I called the base commander at the Naval Air Station at Alameda, California, and he informed me that the planes had already been sold the day before—to a scrap dealer. I got on the phone to this scrap dealer—Hugo Forrester was his name—and determined that he would be happy to sell the four giant boats."

With the blessings of the forest industries joint committee, Dan and three other experts in their field set off the next day for Alameda, where they would evaluate the Mars for its suitability as a water bomber. "Once we saw

those four beauties, we knew they were the aircraft for the job," recalled the pilot. This opinion was shared by the engineers and by the B.C. Forest Service personnel who had accompanied Dan to the Naval Air Station.

The scrap merchant had purchased the planes for the unbelievably low price of $23,000 for all four aircraft. He was prepared to sell the lot for $100,000. Furthermore, he would deliver them in flyable condition, ready for transport. It was planned that they would be flown up to Victoria, where the water tanks would be installed. McIvor and his delegation were ecstatic—but, unbelievably, the joint forest committee turned down the proposal that the Mars be purchased for the job.

Dan McIvor recalled this moment as a low point in the history of aerial

Four of the U.S. Navy's Mars had just been sold for scrap for a meagre $23000. McIvor bought the four from the scrap dealer for $100,000 and the Navy gave him a million dollars worth of spares. Pictured, is one of the giant boats descending the ramp at Alameda, California.

COURTESY USN, ALAMEDA

Facing page: Faiery Aviation, located at Victoria's international airport, stripped the aircraft of unnecessary gear and installed a 7,000-gallon plywood tank with hull-mounted pickup valves.

DAN McIVOR PRESS PHOTO

firefighting. He and his colleagues were devastated. But a salesman-type who overheard the group's plight gave them some good advice at the right moment: "Get off your collective asses and do a selling job on that committee." So McIvor sat down with Duncan McFadden, the secretary of MacMillan Bloedel, and the two men prepared a brief that would become a landmark proposal in the history of the forest industries. On the strength of their detailed proposal, the purchase of the four Martin Mars flying boats was approved.

McIvor jumped back in with renewed enthusiasm to make the deal with the scrap merchant and to prepare the giant boats for their flight to Victoria. While doing so, he was approached by the U.S. Navy stores manager, who advised him that the navy had 35 spare engines for the Mars, and would he like to make an offer for them? McIvor, realizing that he was the only person in the world

PAPER BAG PILOT

with any use for those engines, winced at the ridiculous price he was about to offer.

"Three hundred bucks apiece," he said.

"Wow," said the stores manager, but he agreed to the deal. Dan's management declined to buy all 35 engines and purchased only eight of them. They would rue this decision later, when they realized one couldn't rebuild the Mars engines for less than $50,000, but it must be remembered that these men were all accountants at best, perhaps foresters—but certainly not aviators.

The U.S. Navy personnel at Alameda base loved those Martin Mars flying boats. To them, the big planes were family, and they were imbued with a mystique of invincibility from the many successful wartime flights made to the South Pacific. That these beautiful, faithful giants would be scrapped was an appalling thought. The navy was delighted that their faithful old friends had been saved from the wrecker's axe and would continue to fly. They extended their appreciation of this fact to McIvor when he took off on his first ferry trip to Victoria in the flying boat named "Marianas" Mars. He found the aircraft loaded to the gunwales with nine tons of spares—a small fortune—all for free.

No one knew just how those parts got aboard the aircraft, but they would prove vital, over the years, in keeping the ships flying.

In Victoria, a company by name of Faiery Aviation was waiting for the big planes. Faiery would strip the aircraft down to the basics and install a 7,000-gallon fibreglassed plywood tank to hold the water. Two pick-up probes were also installed in the bottom of the aircraft's hull. These probes were designed to allow the Mars to take on water while step-taxiing on the water.

As the aircraft arrived from California, they were placed on wheeled dollies and stored between two big wartime hangars at the Victoria airport. The "Caroline" Mars was on its dolly one night in 1962 when the tail end of Hurricane Frieda roared through the airport. The wind ripped off the tie-downs and sent the aircraft sailing across the tarmac on its wheeled dolly. It travelled out along a taxiway, and then the dolly struck the edge of the runway. The dolly stopped, but Caroline didn't—she kept on going, crumpling one wing and breaking her back as she came to rest from the last landing of her life. When Caroline was scrapped, workmen found a paper taped to her nose. Some aviator, possessed by a nostalgic muse, had penned the sentiments of all those

"They who must be convinced"—the consortium of forest-industry executives who first turned down the opportunity to buy the four Mars transports. A salesman, or "drummer," as McIvor called him, convinced Dan and accountant Duncan McFadden to renew their efforts and not give up. Together, the two men created a new brief that gained the enthusiastic agreement of the group, and Forest Industries Flying Tankers (FIFT) was born. DAN McIVOR PRESS PHOTO

who had witnessed the demise of this great plane:

> The mocking sky recalls the thunder of your voice,
> Knows you once soared beyond eagles,
> Cast your shadow on treasured South Sea Isles.

Now only three aircraft remained: "Hawaii" Mars, "Philippine" Mars and "The Marianas" Mars. Totally equipped to perform their firefighting job, the three Martins, with crews and maintenance facilities in place, were based at Sproat Lake, near Port Alberni on Vancouver Island. The newly formed industry consortium registered the company as Forest Industries Flying Tankers (FIFT). The behemoths were now ready for business.

The B.C. Forest Service was initially reluctant to call out the Mars because

Ever the feisty adversary of the B.C. Forest Service, Dan McIvor failed to convince them that the Mars, brought to the scene early enough, could extinguish a forest fire, not just control the spread of the flames. On the aircraft's debut as a firefighter, the bombers completely extinguished an outbreak in Belize Inlet. DAN McIVOR PRESS PHOTO

Facing page: The only aircraft capable of putting out a fire single-handed: the Mars can drop 7,000 gallons of water on each pass. The three operational Mars aircraft are credited with saving millions of dollars of British Columbia's timber since their introduction in 1959. DAN McIVOR PRESS PHOTO

PAPER BAG PILOT

Facing page: Two Martin Mars water bombers on Sproat Lake, near Port Alberni, their operational and maintenance base. These aging flying boats face extinction because their maintenance and operating costs exceed the capabilities of a fast-declining industry.

WM. JESSE PHOTO

of the craft's high cost of operation. This was ultimately found to be a short-sighted policy. The sheer impact of that suffocating 70,000 pounds of water put out fires, whereas other methods merely controlled them. Two blazes that occurred during those early days of the Mars, one at nearby Cowichan Lake and the other at Rupert Arm, were stopped dead in their tracks by the early deployment of the Mars water bombers. Never before had such an effective tool been employed against the ravages of forest fires. McIvor's early enthusiasm was entirely vindicated.

Not long after the Mars bombers went into service, tragedy struck. Working a major conflagration at Northwest Bay, near Parksville, the Marianas Mars chose not to dump its load over the target, for reasons unknown. Staggering into a steep, heavily laden turn, the Marianas was denied her usual manoeuvrability and crashed into the mountainside, killing her entire crew. The lessons learned from this accident, and the experience gained from the repeated use of the Mars over the last half-century, has led to an outstanding safety record in what is truly a hazardous business.

Postscript

Dan McIvor is retired now, and rumour is rife that his Mars bombers will soon be joining him. But don't count on McIvor becoming a museum piece along with his aging Mars; he has already come up with a replacement concept: huge, land-based aircraft, such as the C-130 Hercules, equipped with retracting probes that suck up thousands of gallons of lake water while in low-level flight. Think twice before you dismiss this idea—this guy is the father of the Mars, and, after all, he invented the paper bag water bomb.

129

10

KEEPING THE OLD CRATE NEW

The de Havilland Beaver was the definitive bush plane, one for which the aviation industry waited some 25 years. Its concept was developed after de Havilland Canada combined the advice it obtained from experienced bush pilots with its own unique approach to aeronautical design. First flown in 1947, the Beaver marked the beginning of de Havilland's STOL (Short Take-off and Landing) program—just what the bush and coastal seaplane operators had been wanting for years. But, as time went on, there was a problem with the Beaver—although de Havilland stopped building it, the industry never stopped wanting it.

Between 1947 and 1960, de Havilland Canada (DHC) built 1,692 model DHC2 Beaver aircraft. It sold them in 62 countries, but most Beavers went to the U.S. Army Air Corps, and many of these served in the Korean and Vietnam wars. The plane builder then moved on to develop other successful designs. Despite the continuing demand for the Beaver from operators around the world, the plane went out of production in May 1960, when the last machine was delivered to the U.S. Army. Later, de Havilland's president,

Phil Garratt, was in favour of retooling for more Beaver production. He did not have the support of the company directors, however, so the company moved on.

At this point, DHC was on the threshold of some very difficult corporate times. The ownership of the company changed: first sold to the Hawker Siddeley Group, it was ultimately bought back by the government of Canada, which established the firm as a crown corporation. The government didn't like being in the aircraft

Previous page: Two, stock amphibious Beavers, at Port Hardy's airport, wait for the morning fog to burn off. Modifications to the successful 1947 design now include a 3 bladed prop, an alternator replacing the original generator system, an extended cabin interior, more windows, freight doors, baggage and float modifications but that original DHC2 Beaver continues to soldier on into its 58th year.

manufacturing business and wisely made a deal with the Boeing Co. to take over de Havilland. But after five years of ownership, the U.S. aircraft giant negotiated with the Canadian government to take it back—it found DHC's aircraft types were impossible to assimilate into their large aircraft production system. Back home in Canada again, de Havilland became one of the aircraft manufacturers absorbed into the Bombardier group of companies, where it remains to this day. Needless to say, during all of these high-powered boardroom antics nobody was thinking about retooling to produce the lowly Beaver.

To fulfill the manufacturer's obligation to provide engineering and parts support for aircraft that are out of production, de Havilland Canada appointed Viking Air Ltd., of Victoria, B.C., as the exclusive parts manufacturer for the Beaver, the Turbo Beaver and the Single Otter. This action satisfied the legal obligations of the company but did nothing to solve the remarkable demand for these workhorses. As the aircraft approached 50 years of service, there was also an urgent need to upgrade their aging systems with present-day technology. The solution to these problems would have to come from the general aviation industry itself, and it was quick to

happen—chiefly on the west coast, where many Beavers and Otters were in service.

An early entrant in this new industry was Kenmore Air, a Seattle, Washington–based seaplane operator with a large and growing fleet of Beavers. This airline was doing much of its flying into British Columbia's waters, bringing a regular crop of American tourists into the sport fishing camps along the B.C. coast. Kenmore was experiencing some of the shortcomings of the aircraft's design and decided to do something about it. One of these problems was the aircraft's electrical system. The 1947 Beaver had a 50-pound battery, mounted aft of the plane's centre of gravity, supplying electricity to the starter and generator, which were located up front with the engine. The 15 feet of cable carrying this power up to the starter was as thick as your thumb and added a lot of weight to the aircraft. Kenmore pulled that early battery and its cable-and-generator system and replaced it with a small, lighter battery, mounted up front on the firewall, and an alternator replaced that ancient generator. The resulting weight-saving from this modification was significant and provided a much superior electrical system.

Another Kenmore modification solved an aerodynamic stability

Kenmore Air figured large in the initial modifications to the 57-year-old Beaver. Pictured here is part of the flight line at Washington state's Kenmore Air harbour. The first three aircraft are piston-engine-powered Beavers displaying three-bladed props, "bubble" windows and "finlets." Also, Sealand Aviation's extended cabin and Alaska Door kit is installed on all of the aircraft. The fourth aircraft in this line-up is a Turbo Beaver displaying all the Sealand modifications as well as the Viking Air increased-gross-weight kit. Close co-operation exists between all the aviation companies creating modifications for this tireless old bush plane.

COURTESY SEALAND AVIATION

problem that was unique to float-equipped Beavers: in certain manoeuvres, a Beaver's pontoons reduced the effectiveness of the aircraft's vertical stabilizer. More stabilizer surface had to be added to the Beavers that were mounted on pontoons. This additional stabilizer, as supplied by the factory, was called a "skeg." It was attached to the tail-cone area on the underside of the fuselage. Pilots hated skegs because they would become damaged when a fully loaded seaplane's tail went over the dock as it turned out. Again Kenmore went to work and invented what it called "finlets"—little vertical stabilizers attached near the tip of the horizontal tailplane on each side of the aircraft—finlets eliminated the need for the skeg, and those harassed pilots smiled again.

Other, more homely modifications were made by this innovative company. Consider the seats of the factory-produced Beaver: pilots had to load the rear passengers first, and those passengers were required to step over a three-place bench seat located amidships. The back of the bench seat folded down to facilitate this loading, but in practice, if the pilot turned his back, three big loggers would scramble onto the bench seat and would have to be asked to get out in order to allow those two little schoolteachers into the rear seat. The only people I know who

NO NUMBERED RUNWAYS

Facing Page: A variant of the pug-nosed DHC-2 workhorse is the Turbo Beaver. De Havilland Canada built only 62 of these turbine-powered aircraft before moving on to building other types. The aircraft was not commercially viable in its original design, but Viking Air of Victoria, B.C., changed that by restructuring it to carry greater loads.
COURTESY VIKING AIR LTD.

bitch more than pilots are loggers, so this was posing a problem for Kenmore, as it did for every other operator. The problem was solved by splitting the back of the bench seat in two so that either side folded forward—now, only one complaining logger would have to get out.

Those loggers, by the way, had wide shoulders, and three of them seated on that bench seat were a tight fit. Again, Kenmore engineers came to the rescue—they designed "bubble windows," effectively widening the aircraft by five inches on each side, right at shoulder level. And then there was the propeller: the prop, or "club," as pilots referred to it, was originally supplied as a two-bladed model, which imparted considerable vibration to the airframe. Kenmore installed a three-bladed prop, producing the same torque as the original but with considerably less noise and a much smoother operation.

Changes to an aircraft's certified configuration require evaluation, testing and approval from the civil aviation authorities. Although this procedure takes time, patience and considerable paper work, it is well worth the exercise. Once the applicant is rewarded with a Supplementary Type Certificate (STC), it is the exclusive owner of the modification it has developed and benefits financially from

its use by other operators. The Kenmore modifications mentioned here were made available to other maintenance organizations in kit form and have been installed on most Beavers in North America.

Back on Canada's west coast, Viking Air was busy developing a gross-weight modification that increased the useful load of a Pratt & Whitney PT-6 turbine-powered Beaver model called the Turbo Beaver, of which de Havilland built only 62. The increased load-carrying ability of this aircraft made it a commercially viable aircraft, which it had not been when first built by DHC. Viking's modification required structural changes to the wing and fuselage as well as increased displacement of the pontoons and an increase in power. Viking, as the certified DHC representative, also offered Beaver owners the opportunity to have their piston-engine Beaver rebuilt into a certified Turbo Beaver—an amazing achievement, considering the extent of the modifications required.

In Campbell River, B.C., the historic home of some off the biggest floatplane operations of all time, Sealand Aviation created a cabin-extension modification kit for the old bird. This innovation extended the inside length of the Beaver's passenger cabin by about two feet, giving passengers more leg room

Sealand Aviation, based in Campbell River, B.C., developed a cabin-extension kit, adding two feet to the length of the interior cabin and increasing the available light by adding two windows per side to replace the factory's famous "porthole." Access to the Beaver's now roomy cabin is made possible through Sealand's innovative "Alaska Door" modification (facing page). Note the increased size of freight now possible to load in the modified aircraft.

and allowing for a separate freight compartment and the addition of an extra window. Sealand took its modifications a step further by redesigning the Beaver fuselage structure to allow the installation of two huge freight doors. Loads the size of full sheets of plywood can now be carried in Beavers equipped with what Sealand dubbed its "Alaska Door."

A Kelowna, B.C.–based company, AOG Air Support Ltd., invaded

hallowed ground by modifying the leading edge of the Beaver wing. "The wing?" cried astonished Beaver lovers everywhere. "The wing on the Beaver is what makes this airplane such a magnificent aircraft!" AOG also added "fences" on the topside of the wing to direct airflow over the aileron control surfaces during slow flight. The industry was, at first, aghast, but evidence was mounting that the stall characteristics of the Beaver's wing

136

could be extremely dangerous under certain conditions—conditions that rarely occur, but when they do they pose serious problems for the pilot. AOG's wing modifications added significant inherent stability to this magnificent airplane.

While these interesting modifications were being applied to Beavers flying on the coast and throughout North America, operators around the world were looking for new aircraft. There weren't any new Beavers, but there were Beaver wrecks hanging in trees in Korea and Vietnam. Beavers were being retired from military service in every one of those 62 countries originally supplied by de Havilland—and these planes could be made like new, if you were somebody like Al Beaulieu. Al's company, Pacific Aircraft Salvage Ltd., was one of the most active aircraft salvage outfits scouring the world for Beavers. And Al found them in the strangest places—Southeast Asia, the Middle East, North Africa, South America—you name the place, and somewhere one of these

One of the earliest suppliers of rebuilt Beavers on the west coast was Pacific Aircraft Salvage Ltd., whose founder, Al Beaulieu, scoured the world for Beavers and parts. Possessing the factory serial number tag was often all that was needed to allow the rebuilding of the aircraft.

138

freighters and turn piles of twisted metal into the most beautiful Beavers you could imagine—all of them equipped with those Kenmore STCs, the Sealand and Viking modifications, and some with his own specialty features. On one occasion, 12 Beavers in various stages of manufacture were counted in Pacific Aircraft's hangar—the place looked like de Havilland Canada back in 1947. The trick to this rebuild business was to locate the manufacturer's serial tag, which was riveted onto the aircraft at time of manufacture. No matter how bad a wreck it was, if you had that tag you were permitted to rebuild that aircraft from the ground up, with new or certified salvaged parts.

Meanwhile, the Single Otter was undergoing an amazing transformation. A company in Bellingham, Washington, Vazar Aerospace Inc., was successfully repowering the Otter with the famous Pratt & Whitney PT-6 turbine engine. The kit supplied by this designer required only a little modification of the airframe to accept the powerful, lightweight propjet engine, but the effect on the aircraft's performance was outstanding. In Vancouver, John Hill, of Aero Flite Industries, supplying the west coast operators with this Turbo Otter, was responsible for many such turbine conversions of

Canadian icons would be available for sale or destined for the scrap heap. Al once visited a South Seas island and noticed an islander paddling a rather strange-looking canoe equipped with a typical outrigger. On closer inspection, he identified the canoe as a pontoon from a Beaver—a very costly item. Of course, the colourful entrepreneur bought this canoe from the happy islander, who walked away from the deal grinning—certain that he had scored a bargain with this unsuspecting "Gringo."

Al would send the wrecks back to his Vancouver hangar on the decks of

Like the Beaver and Otter aircraft, the Pratt & Whitney PT6 Turbine engine was a Canadian development that revolutionized aircraft power plants the world over. The weight per horsepower of the PT6 made a joke out of the history of aircraft piston engines—their designers long striving to achieve one horsepower per pound of engine.

HEATH MOFFATT PHOTO

A weird-looking modification that worked: the government of Alaska modified this Beaver by adding a Garrett turbine engine. Despite its strange appearance, the aircraft performed well and is still in service.

JIM JORGENSON PHOTO

KEEPING THE OLD CRATE NEW

NO NUMBERED RUNWAYS

What a difference a nose makes! The radial-engine-powered Single Otter (facing page) and Viking Air's PT-6 turbine-powered Otter (right). Many operators prefer the single-turbine machine to its bigger cousin, the Twin Otter, because of its economy of operation, with a performance nearly equal to that of the twin engine machine.

VIKING AIR PHOTO

the "big single." Viking Air, Kenmore and AOG Air Support were each quick to follow this lead and develop their own versions of turbine-powered Otters, and the Canadian engine manufacturer Orenda also offers an in-line piston engine conversion to keep that great airplane flying. Coastal operators were soon showing a preference for the turbine-powered Single Otter over its bigger cousin, the Twin Otter, and for good reason: a reduced cost of operation while carrying nearly the same passenger load. Also, the airplane was quiet, for a change—the piston-powered Single Otter had been so noisy that passengers could neither speak nor be heard during flight, and the pilots who flew this aircraft were destined to be deaf as a post in their golden years. The new turbine versions were whisper-quiet.

NO NUMBERED RUNWAYS

Facing page: One of the early modifications to the Single Otter was the installation of a 1000 horsepower Polish engine with four-bladed prop. The resulting rate of climb is spectacular. Pictured here in the Vancouver hangar of Aero Flite Industries is an American registered amphibious Otter with the big engine conversion and redesigned floats allowing for additional loading.

JIM JORGENSON PHOTO

Harrison Ford's personal Beaver is shown here under rebuild at Kenmore Air's Seattle hangar. The Hollywood actor's Beaver is a stock machine and is flown on wheels. The question remains: can the old bird handle celebrity?

COURTESY KENMORE AIR

While all this upgrading was going on, something else was happening to change the venerable Beaver for all time: it was being priced out of its useful market. Who could fly groceries and flats of beer into logging camps with a $500,000 airplane? From a 1947 price of $30,000 to a half-million dollars was a big leap. As one operator noted, it's all very well to own a half-million-dollar airplane, but it's not worth a dime if nobody wants to buy it! When movie star Harrison Ford bought a Beaver from Kenmore Air, the message came through loud and clear:

that Canadian masterpiece, that humble, old, beloved crate, had gone to Hollywood. This rise to stardom posed the question: will celebrity ruin the de Havilland Beaver? We think not. The aircraft remains the engineering triumph of the century—more the Canadian icon than the RCMP's "musical ride," and the dream of "coast dogs" of every generation. Watch for it landing on a small lake near you.

143